SUSAN J FOSTER

Righteous Rage

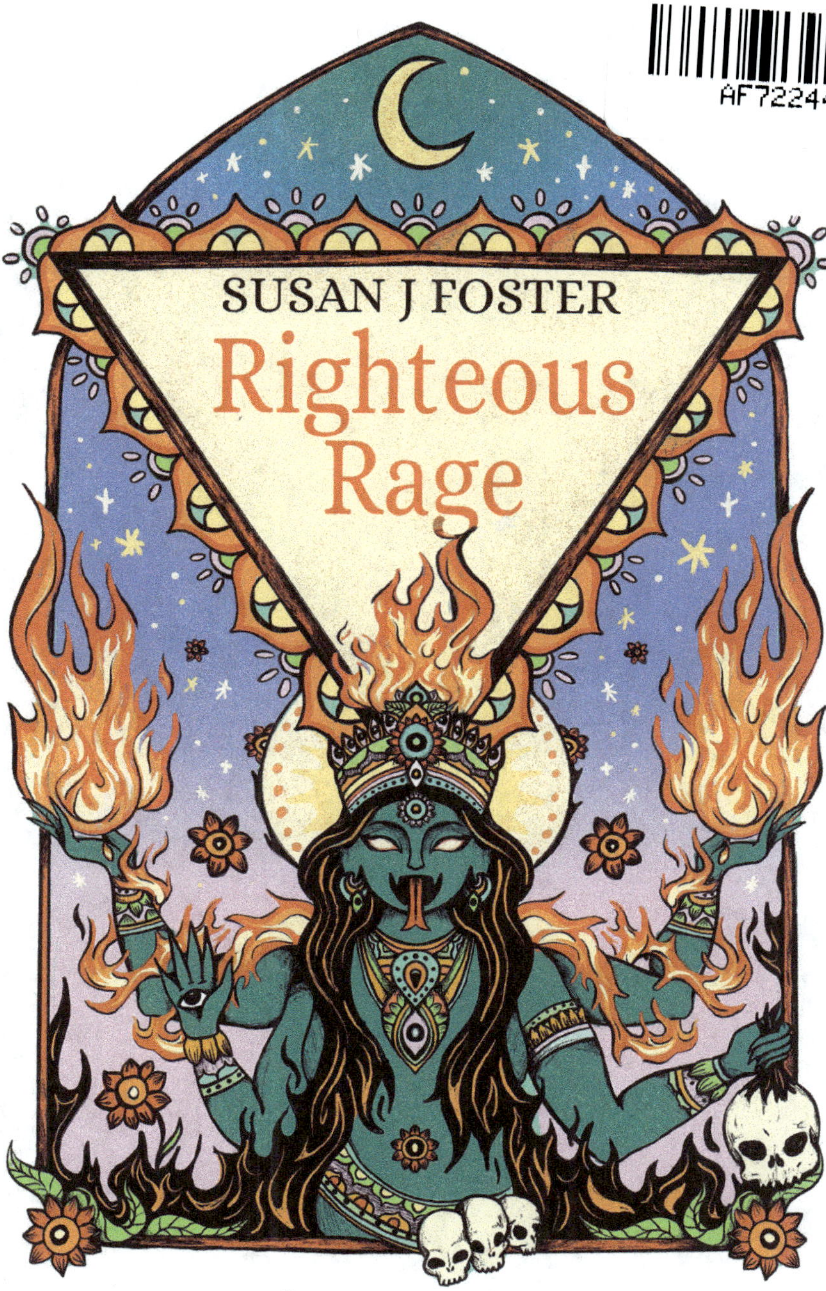

Why Feminism Needs the Fierce Goddesses

CHIRON PUBLICATIONS • ASHEVILLE, NORTH CAROLINA

Praise for *Righteous Rage: Why Feminism Needs the Fierce Goddesses*

"In *Righteous Rage*, Susan Foster does more than chronicle the trajectory of American feminism—she revitalizes its essence with intellectual depth, lived experience, and a spiritually grounded Jungian perspective. Drawing upon her personal evolution and the enduring archetypes of the fierce goddess, Foster follows in the lineage of thinkers like Esther Harding and Soraya Chemaly to assert a crucial truth: female rage is not dangerous—it is sacred, transformational, and urgently needed.

For too long, patriarchal culture has met this rage with fear, ridicule, and suppression. Foster contends that reclaiming it is key to personal healing and dismantling systems of injustice. Both incisive and restorative, this book blends memoir, feminist scholarship, and psychological insight in ways that challenge the male-biased frameworks of traditional science and medicine.

With clarity and conviction, *Righteous Rage* confronts the entrenched forces of patriarchy, racism, and silencing—and invites readers to awaken their fierce wisdom. It is a galvanizing call to action: embrace your power, wield it purposefully, and fight for a world worthy of our full voices.

In *Righteous Rage*, Susan Foster's herstory matters. She reminds us that women instinctively come together in times of trauma. In a world where that trauma is ongoing and systemic, our collective rage is not only justified, it is essential. This is not new. Across cultures and centuries, women have drawn upon the deep memory of matriarchal traditions—where rage was sacred, a force for justice that needed no armies, no militarized state, no corrupt hierarchies of man-made law.

Foster understands rage as more than emotion: it is an ancient survival mechanism encoded in our DNA, ready to be transformed into healing and evolution. This book reclaims that inheritance with power and clarity. *Righteous Rage* is a fierce, visionary work—part invocation, part roadmap—offering readers radical permission to remember, to resist, and to rise."

-Danica Anderson, author of *South Slavic Women's Trans-generational Trauma Healing Through Oral Memory Practices*

"Susan Foster has written a book for all American women, a vivid mosaic intertwining vignettes of the fierce divine female through time and space with the need for a new feminist rage against patriarchal demonization of the female in our world today."

-Lora Holland, Professor Emerita of UNC Asheville, author of "Cervidology and the Antlered Deer of Artemis: Representation Between Myth and Reality," Memoirs of the American Academy in Rome 68 (2023), JSTOR.

"*Righteous Rage* is a juicy book for our times, when women's frustration, anger, and rage at the patriarchal powers that be have reached yet another boiling point. Susan Foster nimbly combines feminist history with stories of the dark or fierce goddesses of various cultures to help us understand where our rage originates and why it matters today. These fierce goddesses are with us showing us how to claim our power in the name of love."

-Stephanie Anderson Ladd, author of *Goddesses of Self-Care: 30 Divine Feminine Archetypes To Guide Us*

"Righteous rage, ancient and modern, a stay against cruelty and violation, a force to be reckoned with."

-Patricia Reis, author of *Through the Goddess: A Woman's Way of Healing* and *Daughters of Saturn: From Father's Daughter to Creative Woman*

www.ChironPublications.com

Interior and cover design by Danijela Mijailovic
Cover art by Erika Busse
Printed primarily in the United States of America.

ISBN 978-1-68503-580-8 paperback
ISBN 978-1-68503-581-5 hardcover
ISBN 978-1-68503-582-2 electronic
ISBN 978-1-68503-583-9 limited edition paperback
ISBN 978-1-68503-584-6 limited edition hardcover

Library of Congress Cataloging-in-Publication Data Pending

“It was … anger at injustice that was the impetus for creating a women’s liberation movement.”

bell hooks

Acknowledgements

My first thanks go to my developmental editor Deborah Steinberg, whose editorial experience and expertise improved my book immeasurably. She restructured it in ways that contributed to its readability and logical coherence. She also suggested additions that turned out to be some of the strongest sections of the book. Her positive feedback was a constant source of motivation that kept me writing for 2 ½ years, even through Hurricane Helene and a move. It was inspirational to work with her as a sister in solidarity with the goals of my project in these challenging times. I am also grateful for the superb job of copy editing by Rob Mikulak, whom I knew to be an excellent editor from the time we worked together at Asheville's alt-weekly newspaper.

Many thanks to Chiron Press for publishing my book and especially to general manager Jennifer Fitzgerald, who tirelessly guided me through the intricacies, and often the confusing landscape, of publishing my first book. I am deeply grateful to Chiron for helping me get this book into the world, where I hope it will make a difference.

A special thanks to Katie Hoffner, the niece of artist Lydia Ruyle, who gave me permission to use images of Lydia's remarkable goddess banners in the book. When Lydia was alive she graciously loaned me a box of her banners to hang during a women's spirituality event I sponsored; their magical energy was transformative for all who viewed them. My hope is that publishing her images will keep Lydia's legacy and her love for the goddesses alive.

I am especially grateful to my friend and Asheville artist Erika Busse for the amazing cover art and images of many of the African and Afro-Caribbean goddesses. I was glad to support Erika's work since her studio was destroyed during Helene and she was, like many Asheville artists, struggling to survive. But I was the lucky one, as her images turned out to be knockouts and added greatly to the appeal of the book.

My heartfelt thanks to my children Heather and Jeremy Foster and my son-in-law Adam Ezring for their unfailing support in my endeavor and for listening to all my updates about its progress ad nauseum. The book is better because of all the probing questions they asked, which contributed immensely to a greater clarity, as well as a deeper development, of my ideas. And finally, a shout-out to my friend Sherry Lundquist for suggesting the catchy title.

I have a huge debt of gratitude to all these people, without whom this work would not have been possible.

Dedicated to my mother
My original fierce goddess

Table of Contents

Introduction

I have never been an angry person. I grew up in the Midwest in the 1950s, when girls and women were expected to be demure and accommodating, never angry. Parents in white, middle-to upper-middle-class families like my own taught their daughters to be "ladies"—polite, ankles crossed when seated, donning white gloves for church or at the slightest hint of a formal occasion. Well-mannered children and adolescents simply did not get angry. Anger was not just considered unladylike; it was considered a moral weakness. "Good" girls were pleasant and passive; they took care of others and denied their own needs. Girls who expressed anger were labeled as "bad;" if they asserted themselves, they were deemed brash and selfish.

My religious upbringing took place in an Episcopal church; there were no images of female deities, just Jesus on the cross. Even the Virgin Mary had an auxiliary role, unlike in the Catholic Church, which venerates her in many of its practices. It was not until I was in my 30s that I discovered goddesses from other spiritual traditions.

I went away to a women's college on the East Coast, hoping to escape the repressive atmosphere of my upbringing. But in those days women's colleges operated *in loco parentis,* with strict curfews and rules about men in dorm rooms (only on Sunday afternoons, with the door open as wide as a book, which we got around by using matchbooks). We were required to wear skirts to dinner and when making trips into the local town. Dorms had "house mothers" who enforced the social conditioning we had experienced before college. My house mother chose me, from all the girls in the dorm, to lead guided tours of the college, undoubtedly because I was a paragon of feminine virtue—pleasant, polite, unassuming, concerned with the needs and feelings of prospective students and their families. I was a representative of the values and privileges of white, upper-middle class families. In my class of 500 students, there was only one Black student, and she was so light skinned that no one even realized she was Black.

Meanwhile, the Vietnam War was raging, and protests were erupting across the nation. Four protesters at Kent State University were shot to death by the Ohio National Guard. I did a stint of draft counseling to register my objection to the war. I stood outside draft centers and offered advice about avoiding the draft to the men who were reporting to register. Our graduating class invited antiwar activist the Rev. William Sloane Coffin to give the baccalaureate service at graduation. However, the college forbade the wearing of armbands or any other symbols of protest against the war. People were dying every day in the war, but as "good girls," we were not allowed to show any signs of indignation.

At this time, abortion for all women and contraceptives for single women were not legal.[1] Hundreds if not thousands of women died every year from illegal abortions.

I never needed to have an abortion, thankfully, but I remember the time I went to a doctor's office in Boston to obtain

---

[1] Married women were legally permitted access to contraceptives in 1965 in Griswold v. Connecticut, but single women did not gain access until 1972 in Eisenstadt v. Baird.

birth control pills. I had gotten the doctor's name from a fellow student. It was a shady and shameful experience, walking into the dark, dingy office of a foreign-national doctor who spoke poor English. He gave me a pelvic exam without anyone else present in the examining room, which ran contrary to standard medical practice and created more than a little fear and suspicion in me. Still, I did not get angry at having to use such a clandestine means to protect myself from an unwanted pregnancy, which would have disrupted my college career if not my entire life.

After graduation I moved to Berkeley, California, where the social revolution of the '60s was happening. Sex, drugs, and rock'n'roll dominated the era, replacing the social conditioning of our childhoods. The Black Panthers were mobilizing, and psychedelic drugs were rampant. I decided to join an antiwar protest on Telegraph Avenue, the street where I lived, in part because of curiosity. Columns of police advanced on protesters and threw tear gas canisters at them. My eyes stung and watered from the tear gas. When the police called for the protesters to disperse, my boyfriend and I fled quickly but were chased by a policeman down alleys and cornered at a fence. He beat my boyfriend with his stick, causing his glasses to fall off and break. The chase and assault left me terrified but not angry. My "good girl" upbringing left me unable to muster anger even at such police brutality.

The next couple of decades of my life were spent furthering my education, starting a career, and raising a family. During this time significant progress on women's rights occurred. The second wave of feminism took off,[2] emphasizing equality in all spheres of domestic and public life, and in 1973 the Supreme

[2] The first wave began in 1848 at the Seneca Falls convention, which focused on property rights and the right to vote.

Court case of Roe v. Wade established the right to abortion. I began to attend a church that offered a course called "Cakes for the Queen of Heaven," which introduced me to the history and images of goddess figures. A whole new religious paradigm opened up to me when I realized that the divine had feminine as well as masculine aspects. The book *When God Was a Woman* by Merlin Stone revolutionized my theology, as I learned that god had been conceived of as female in many prepatriarchal cultures. I immediately became a part of the goddess movement, familiarizing myself with many female deities, including the fierce goddesses, whose vigorous energy was exercised in support of social justice. In reading about prepatriarchal societies that honored the goddess, I learned that such societies operated on a partnership model rather than a patriarchal model that oppresses both men and women because it locks them both into prescribed gender roles.

My educational pursuits during this phase of my life led to my becoming a clinical psychologist, but despite my training and practice of psychology, it was not until the presidential debate in 2016 that my anger really began to surface. I was disgusted as I watched the presidential debate between Hillary Clinton and Donald Trump. He lurked behind her like a diabolical ghost sent to haunt her. Trump, a self-described harasser of women who bragged about "grabbing women by the pussy" in the *Access Hollywood* tape, was totally unapologetic about his harassment of women. During the campaign, Trump called Clinton "the devil" and "a nasty woman." His contagious chant of "Lock Her Up" made me incensed. I stayed up half the night to see our first woman elected as president and went to bed in tears (a common way for women to express their anger). Trump's victory added insult to injury, as it was a win for white supremacist, misogynist culture.

Like many others who couldn't believe the results as they came in, my anger hit the decibel level. It escalated into rage when Trump appointed Amy Coney Barrett to the Supreme Court, ostensibly to overturn the 1973 case of Roe v. Wade. When the Supreme Court did just that with the 2022 case of Dobbs v. Jackson Women's Health Organization, and women's rights to their own bodily autonomy were trashed, I was so enraged that I didn't know what to do. Confronted with the suffering of women forced to endure pregnancies they don't want or pregnancies they do want but are not viable because of fetal anomalies, I could no longer contain my anger.

I decided to write a book about women's rage, because I felt compelled to take some kind of action, and for me the pen is mightier than the sword. My rage became the motivation for writing this book. Rage can serve as motivation to take action to create systems that are more just. I have come to realize that anger is a justifiable response to an unjust action. When anger and rage are harnessed appropriately, they can serve as fuel for the fight to dismantle patriarchy, racism, and classism.

Once I made friends with my anger, I felt the fierce goddesses calling to me across the ages with an urgent message I knew I had to share. It was as if they came to me in a dream, trying to communicate the need to connect with our sacred rage to fight patriarchy and its related ills.

These goddesses, or archetypes as they are sometimes referred to in Jungian terms, carry a profound wisdom for women throughout time, regardless of their circumstances. The fierce, or dark, goddesses have lived in what Jung calls the shadow—the unintegrated parts of our psyches that we are not normally conscious of. If we can excavate them from the deepest parts of our psyches, we can connect to our innate sense of courage and inner power. They will help us fight the good fight against injustice, transforming paradigms that have kept all of us, men and women alike, oppressed. As archetypes, they live within all of us. They are a liberatory force for all people in all cultures. The various goddesses have different aspects which I will explore in this book. But drawing on their fierce natures is the key to transforming those parts of ourselves and of society that no longer serve us.

This book is not a comprehensive survey of all fierce goddesses. Rather, I have chosen certain fierce goddesses to illustrate how they can lend their energy and strength to the fight for justice. The book will focus on American feminism and issues faced by American feminists, not feminism from around the world or in different cultures. However, feminist struggles in other countries or cultures can serve as inspiration for American feminists, and this book includes some of these as examples.

For purposes of this discussion, I will not attempt to define the word "woman" but will use the term to include all people who identify as women—transwomen and nonbinary individuals as well as biological females. Whenever I use the word "woman," it will be understood to refer to all those who identify as women. Transmen do not identify as women, but as female-bodied people, they face many of the same reproductive health issues as women.

Let us, then, take a journey within to discover the latent parts of ourselves that can heal us and propel us forward into a more enlightened, just world.

CHAPTER ONE

What Is Feminism?

"Ain't I a Woman?"—Sojourner Truth

The recent backlash against feminism, highlighted by the Supreme Court's decision in Dobbs v. Jackson Women's Health Organization on June 24, 2022, which overturned Roe v. Wade and revoked federal the right to abortion, has left many people asking: Is feminism dead? Or if it isn't dead, is it lost?

When discussing the feminist movement, the initial question must be: What is feminism? Merriam-Webster's Dictionary defines feminism as the belief in and advocacy of political, economic, and social equality between men and women. In contrast, American author and social critic bell hooks defines feminism as "a movement to end sexism, sexist exploitation, and oppression" (hooks, 2000). This definition emphasizes sexist thinking and action, whether perpetuated by men or women. Women as well as men can be sexist, she claims. Her definition also points to sexism as an institutionalized form of oppression, apart from individual actions.

The problem with hooks' definition, however, is that it begs the question of what sexism is. If feminism is a movement to eradicate sexism, conceived simply in opposition to sexism, then what is sexism? Without an adequate definition of sexism, we cannot give clear voice to what feminism is. According to hooks, sexism is a system of oppression that results in disadvantages for women, favoring the rights, privileges, and opportunities of men over those of women. Defining feminism in contrast to sexism means it is a movement aimed at removing inequalities between the sexes. A sexist system, although it materially and legally privileges men, still oppresses them by confining them to certain roles and expectations (e.g., stay-at-home dads are often looked down upon as shirking their financial responsibilities as fathers).

In practice, feminism has shifted and grown through different eras, or "waves." The first wave of feminism, which grew out of the Seneca Falls conference in 1848, was largely a movement by suffragists to eliminate inequality between the sexes based on the right to vote. For several decades women lobbied and protested for the right to vote, in some cases with hunger strikes and civil disobedience. In 1878, the 19th Amendment to the U.S. Constitution was introduced in Congress; it read: "The right of citizens of the United States to vote shall not be denied or abridged by the United States or by any State on account of sex." The amendment was not ratified until 1920, when 36 states passed it, and women finally got the right to vote.

Second wave feminism, which took place in the 1960s and '70s, focused on a variety of other inequalities, including the wage gap, job opportunities and hiring practices, and specific rights that women lacked—owning property, divorcing, holding political office, and pursuing higher education. It also espoused reproductive rights, sexual freedom, and safety from domestic violence and rape. Third wave feminism, occurring from the 1990s to the 2010s, took up issues of diversity and intersectionality.

The Equal Rights Amendment, which reads, "Equality of rights under the law shall not be denied or abridged by the

United States or by any state on account of sex," was drafted in 1923 by two suffragists, Alice Paul and Crystal Eastman. It was proposed as a constitutional amendment designed to remove inequalities and give women the same constitutional protections as men. Passage by 38 states was required, and although that number was eventually reached, the 1982 deadline for passage had already expired, and several states rescinded their support, leaving the ERA in limbo. It has still not been ratified.

Some of the inequalities the ERA attempted to address have been remedied by other laws. For instance, wage disparities were dealt with by the Massachusetts Equal Pay Act of 2018, which outlawed wage discrimination on the basis of gender. The Equal Pay Act of 1963, signed into law by President Kennedy, prohibited sex discrimination by employers involved in commerce or the production of goods for commerce. The Lilly Ledbetter Fair Pay Act of 2009 made further headway regarding equal pay and is discussed in more detail in Chapter Eight. And the Paycheck Fairness Act of 2021 addressed wage discrimination on the basis of gender, including pregnancy, sexual orientation, and gender identity.

Another area of discrimination that the ERA would have prohibited is sexual harassment, which was made illegal by Title VII of the Civil Rights Act of 1964 for employers with more than 15 employees as well as the federal government. The Anti-Sexual Harassment Act of 1995 gave a definition of sexual harassment that included pressure for sexual favors and unwelcome comments about appearance.

Discrimination against women undergoing divorce would have been covered by the ERA, but other laws have been passed to address the issue. In 1969, California adopted no-fault divorce, signed into law by then-Governor Ronald Reagan; other states followed suit. Previously, women had to provide substantial proof that their husbands had committed adultery in order to be granted a divorce, but courts were biased toward men. Even in cases in which divorce was granted to women, there were no legal requirements for equal division of assets or financial support, often leaving women in poverty. Custody of children was uniformly given to fathers, a further erosion of women's rights. The upshot of such practices was that women were often afraid to leave unhappy or abusive marriages.

The New York State Married Women's Property Act of 1848 had made it easier for women to claim property and marital assets, and other states had subsequently passed similar laws mandating that women be allowed to own property, control their own wages, and enter into contracts. Although Married Women's Property Acts in some states liberalized women's economic rights, they did not outlaw marital rape (which was legal in all states before the 1970s) or give women the right to have custody of their children. Although gains have been made in such areas, passage of the ERA would presumably have given full protection from the outset.

Although establishing legal equality with men is a laudable goal of feminism, and many gains have been made without passage of the ERA—especially with respect to wage discrimination, sexual harassment, and divorce proceedings—full equality will be achieved only when the ERA is passed, removing many extant barriers to equality.

However, defining feminism as a movement to establish social and political equality with men is limiting, in that such equality cannot establish the full extent of women's rights. Establishing equality with men leaves open the possibility that women's rights may be reduced if men's rights are abridged by the legal system. For example, an oppressive political system that revoked rights currently granted to men would by extension revoke women's rights as well, while still maintaining women's equality with men. In many totalitarian societies, human rights violations occur across the board without regard to sex—notably restrictions on freedom of speech and religion, along with unfair arrests and freedom from arbitrary arrest. Denying women such rights is surely inconsistent with feminism, even though they may be on equal footing with men. And from a theoretical standpoint, if men ceased to exist (perhaps wiped out by a gender-specific plague) and as a result laws that pertained to them were revoked, the proper benchmark for feminism could not be equality with men. The same could be said about a society consisting solely of women.

A feminist perspective could further argue that women are entitled to certain rights regardless of whether those rights are equally granted to men. For instance, if a repressive regime targeted only men (unlikely but theoretically possible) by imprisoning them for their political or religious beliefs, feminism would seek to preserve such freedoms for women and would not be content with equality to men.

Another problem with defining feminism solely as a movement to establish equality with men is that women may require certain rights to which men have no comparable right—rights that only women can enjoy. For example, even though men and women may both be granted bodily integrity by the legal system under the U.S. Fourth Amendment, which calls for "the right of people to be secure in their persons," men have no comparable right to bodily integrity when pregnant (except in the case of transgender men, who face the same situation in regard to bodily integrity as cisgendered women while pregnant). Being a man, even legally, would not grant additional protection from prosecution for having an abortion. The ability to carry another life in one's body necessitates another level of additional legal protections. If women have the right to bodily integrity while carrying a fetus (as was the case before Roe v. Wade was overturned in 2022), such a case is more nuanced and involves many more considerations than a case of bodily integrity for men, which by necessity cannot involve issues of another life growing within their bodies. In this sense the right to abortion is a right that only women or female-bodied people can have, and feminism advocates for this right, regardless of whether men have any comparable or equal right. Similarly, rights to oral contraceptives, IUDs, and the morning-after pill—all of which are currently being reexamined in the wake of the Dobbs case—are not rights that men can be said to have.

So, a framework that explains feminism in terms of achieving social and legal equality with men is at best incomplete. How, then, can we define feminism in a way that does not depend solely on women achieving equality with men?

The 1995 Fourth World Conference on Women in Beijing, held on the 50th anniversary of the founding of the United Nations, set out a global platform for action to ensure "the advancement and empowerment of women all over the world." The platform called for elimination of discrimination against women and the removal of obstacles to gender equality so that women could enjoy "full participation on the basis of equality in all spheres of society," including "equal rights, opportunities and access to resources," as well as "equal sharing of responsibilities for the family by men and women." However, the platform did not limit its action imperatives to achieving equality with men. It also called for "the full implementation of the human rights of women … as an inalienable, integral and indivisible part of all human rights and fundamental freedoms." Championing women's rights as human rights establishes certain rights as inalienable—meaning they are fundamental to the status of women as human beings, inherent in their human dignity, and thus cannot justifiably be abridged or revoked by any political system. The platform gives as examples "the right to freedom of thought, conscience, religion, and belief."

The Beijing Declaration provides for a better, more expansive, understanding of what feminism is, as it calls for the protection of certain inalienable rights as well as the achievement of equality with men on various social and economic measures. Using language from the Beijing Declaration, a definition of feminism that advocates for the advancement and empowerment of women (and that includes not only the removal of obstacles to full social and economic equality with men but also the inalienable rights possessed by women) is a fuller and more complete definition. Of course, such a definition leaves open the full extent of which rights may be counted as inalienable, and feminists themselves may disagree on this question, but it does provide a starting point for discussing different forms of feminism.

The three current major forms of feminism are liberal or mainstream, radical, and socialist or Marxist. Liberal feminism, the oldest of the "Big Three" forms of feminism, had its origin in first wave feminism and focused on reforms within a democratic framework that promote social change within existing institutions. It advocated for individual rights and legislative protections for women, especially the rights to vote and pursue higher education.

By contrast, radical feminism, which emerged during the second wave, is a revolutionary social justice movement that calls for the dismantling of patriarchal institutions. It identifies the domination of women by men under the patriarchal system as the root cause of women's oppression, as opposed to liberal feminism, which advocates for equal legal rights within the current system. Some radical feminists, known as TERFs (trans-exclusionary radical feminists), disavow participation in the women's movement by transwomen, claiming they are not women. Determining who counts as a woman has been a divisive issue within the feminist movement of late.

Socialist, or Marxist, feminism, which began in the 1930s, almost 100 years after Karl Marx analyzed the ways in which patriarchy and capitalism are intertwined, became popular in the 1960s and '70s; it held that the capitalist system, under which much of women's labor is uncompensated, is complicit in the oppression of women. Marx identified racism and class exploitation, alongside sexism, as factors contributing to social injustice.

Aside from these three major forms of feminism, there are many variations of feminism, including cultural feminism, Black feminism, choice feminism, and ecofeminism. Cultural feminism posits essential differences between men and women based on biological differences. Black feminism centers the experiences of African American women and looks at the interplay of racism and sexism in society. Ecofeminism compares the oppression of women to the defilement of the environment as a result of patriarchy and capitalism. Intersectional feminism is a type of feminism that refers, according to the Oxford English Dictionary, to the "interconnected nature of social categorizations such as race, class, and gender, ...regarded as creating overlapping and interdependent systems of discrimination or advantage" (Oxford English Dictionary. languages.oup.com. n.d.). Intersectional feminism will be discussed in more depth in Chapter Three, and this book in general takes an intersectional approach to feminism.

Choice feminism, by contrast, holds that the purpose of women's liberation is to give all women as many choices as possible within society and to validate all choices as stemming from women's freedom. It validates a woman's choice to be a stay-at-home mother or to pursue a career. The term "choice feminism" was coined by Linda Hirshman in 2006 to criticize the "free choice" of housewives who sacrificed their careers for a more traditional gender role. On the face of it, giving women the power to make such decisions for themselves sounds good. Women who choose to be homemakers and caretakers of children should not be judged for their choice or made to feel that they are any less "feminist" because of it. Similarly, a woman who chooses to pursue a career can be respected for her choice as well. Isn't giving women choices about how to live their lives a fundamental tenet of feminism? Yes and no.

One criticism of choice feminism stems from the fact that women who are marginalized in society, whether due to poverty, race, or class, may not have the same economic and educational opportunities as more privileged women. What sense does it make to reduce feminism to the ability to make choices when social and economic circumstances limit the choices of many women? For instance, a young woman who grew up in poverty and had to quit school to help support her family does not have the same choice to attend an Ivy League school as a woman whose family was wealthy and paid for private schools for her. But choice feminism is riddled with more problems than simple limitations of choice.

Although expanding women's choices may seem like a laudable goal, there may be some choices that are incompatible with feminism. For instance, if a woman decides not just to be a homemaker and mother but also to marry an "alpha" male with the intention of being subservient to him, can she be said to be a feminist? If she organizes her life around forgoing her own needs and serving those of her husband and children, is she truly a feminist? If she gives her husband, as the head of the household, complete decision-making authority over the children and herself, then she has revoked her own power and conformed to patriarchal norms for the family unit. Yes, she has made her own choice to be governed by such norms, but they are incompatible with feminism.

The appointment of Amy Coney Barrett to the Supreme Court has raised the question of whether she is a feminist. Some writers have claimed that she is an example of a new form of feminism, combining motherhood (of seven children, two of whom are adopted) with a high-powered legal career. She is regarded as a woman who can "have it all" and maintain work-life balance at the same time. But while she has been successful in both the domestic and career arenas, that is not enough to qualify her as a feminist.

Barrett is a member of a charismatic religious sect known as "People of Praise," which espouses the belief that women are subordinate to men and that women need permission from their husbands to pursue careers. A 2010 People of Praise directory lists Barrett as a "handmaid," a leadership role for women who served as advisers to other women (Brown, 2020). The group stopped using the term after the popularity of the Hulu series "The Handmaid's Tale," which premiered in 2016 and was based on Margaret Atwood's 1985 book of the same name. Atwood said her book was based on groups such as People of Praise.

Adrian Reimers, one of the founders of People of Praise who later left, wrote in his book *Not Reliable Guides* that the subordination of women is a cultural premise of the group and that a married woman is always under her husband's authority:

> The wife, as a good member of the community, has a prima facie obligation to obey her husband as the bearer of God's will. In practice, this means that the two do not—indeed, cannot—relate as equals. His will reveals God's to her, whereas her will is merely human. The

> two cannot meet as equals, because the husband always has divine authority on his side. (Reimers, 2017)

In embracing such sexist beliefs espoused by People of Praise, Barrett cannot be considered a feminist. Regarding a husband as the spiritual head and authority of his wife runs counter to the feminist principle of equality between men and women. Despite her spectacular success as a career woman, making it all the way to the Supreme Court, Barrett has aligned herself with the patriarchy and its noxious view of women as subordinate. Even though she has made a choice to live her life according to the beliefs and practices of People of Praise, her choice alone does not confer a label of choice feminism.

Choice may simply be an illusion for women like Barrett, who have been conditioned by their religion to accept patriarchal norms. They might be considered brainwashed into following their religion's strictures, or at least programmed into embracing them. They are likely to face social judgment in their families and religious organizations for not following prescribed gender roles, making authentic choice illusory.

Furthermore, Barrett's long-standing antiabortion stance, as reflected in her vote to abolish the right to abortion in the Dobbs decision, also disqualifies her from being a feminist. I agree with hooks' perspective that a woman cannot be antiabortion and also a feminist: "If feminism is a movement to end sexist oppression, and depriving females of reproductive rights is a form of sexist oppression, then one cannot be anti-choice and be feminist" (hooks, 2000). Supporting patriarchal norms, even when chosen, and denying females reproductive rights rule out being a feminist.

As the current backlash against feminism gains traction, feminist authors increasingly report a retrenchment of the movement. Kiara Barrow and Rebecca Panovka recently published a series of essays in their journal, *The Drift*. In their introduction, Barrow and Panovka wrote, "For a long time now, we've had the sense that feminism is in trouble." The articles in the collection, titled "What to Do About Feminism," point to a lack of vitality, a sense of stagnancy, in the movement. "We're quite alarmed to see that the people around us … are by and large quite disaffected and maybe considered themselves feminists five years ago," says Panovka, "but now don't want to anymore" (Barrow & Panovka, 2022).

Earlier this year, the Southern Poverty Law Center and Tulchin research conducted a poll of 1,500 Americans. A majority of Republican men under 50 (62%) agreed with the statement "Feminism has done more harm than good," and 42% of Republican men over 50 also agreed. By contrast, 46% of Democratic men under 50 and 4% of Democratic men over 50 agreed. Although women in general agreed less, nevertheless 52% of Republican women under 50 and 51% of their older counterparts agreed, as well as 23% of Democratic women under 50 and 10% of those over 50. These numbers substantiate the claim that feminism is in serious trouble and do not bode well for the future of feminism (Southern Poverty Law Center, 2022).

The fierce goddesses of ancient times have the potential to reinvigorate feminism if we look to them for inspiration and guidance. Their potent energy can serve as fuel to revive a flagging feminist movement or hopefully ignite another wave of feminism.

CHAPTER TWO

Who Are the Fierce Goddesses?

"Darkness precedes the light and she is Mother."
— Salerno Cathedral, Italy

With so much antipathy and apathy toward feminism, how can feminism move forward? How can it be revitalized to regain its momentum? The answer may lie in the distant past, long before the feminist movement as such took form. The "fierce goddesses" of ancient times represent an archetype of female rage against injustice.

This archetype has been laid down in the deep recesses of our psyches—in what psychiatrist Carl Jung calls the collective unconscious. If we allow our psyches to explore the dark, or shadow, side of the unconscious, images of the fierce goddesses can emerge. These fierce goddesses, who are also known as "dark goddesses," carry a primordial energy of destruction of those systems and paradigms that no longer serve us. The dark goddesses challenge paradigms that need to be destroyed, especially patriarchy, which has effectively pushed them into the shadow. They also have the power to create new, nonpatriarchal structures that promote well-being and align with justice. The dark goddesses of ancient times have been submerged in our psyches, but they serve as a repository of fierce energy, of female rage against injustice, which, if tapped into, can rejuvenate the flagging women's movement.

Hecate

One of the best-known dark goddesses is Hecate (also spelled Hekate). Although she is usually identified as a Greek goddess, appearing frequently in Greek myths, she actually predates Greek mythology, originating in the Carian culture of Asia Minor. Her mother and father were the second-generation Titans Perses and Asteria. The Titans ruled over the earth before they were defeated by the Olympians. Zeus defeated his Titan father, Cronus, and banished most of the Titans. Hecate was one of the few Titans whom Zeus allowed to retain her powers on Mount Olympus.

Unlike the other gods and goddesses who lived on Mount Olympus, however, Hecate chose to live in a cave. She preferred the underground darkness to the light-filled summit of Olympus. She is a chthonic goddess—one who belongs to or inhabits the underworld. Her cave is the womb from which we emerge and eventually return to in death. To enter her cave is to undergo the mystery of transformation through life, death, and rebirth. When we descend into her cave, we encounter the darkness of our shadows, which enables us to claim the parts of ourselves that lie latent, but fertile, within us. The Underworld journey is necessary for us to become whole, individuated selves. Chthonic goddesses such as Hecate carry a message to contemporary feminists about the importance of getting in touch with our shadow sides; they guide us into the Underworld to undergo transformation that leads to becoming whole.

When patriarchy established a monotheistic male sky god, Hecate's cave, in the subterranean depths of the earth, came to be seen as evil. Later chapters will discuss how patriarchal religions

Hecate

Art and image © Lydia Ruyle.

reviled many of the fierce, or dark, goddesses. But it's important to remember that Hecate, despite being vilified by patriarchal religions, is a benevolent goddess, both protector and healer, who helps us move into wholeness.

Hecate is referred to in the Chaldean Oracles, philosophical writings from the third to sixth century C.E., as the Anima Mundi, the female soul of the world, which reigns over both creation and destruction as archetypal mother (many fierce goddesses from different cultures embody this union of creation and destruction). Hesiod describes Hecate as a goddess who oversees all that is (Brannen, 2023). She is known as the keeper of the keys; she unlocks the gates to the deepest and most profound mysteries of the universe. As the mediator between the mundane and the sacred, she removes all obstacles to our descent into the fertile darkness of her womb, where transformation takes place.

Hecate holds two torches which guide our way through the darkness into her cave. Her torches have become one of her identifying markers. Hecate is referred to as Phosphoros (light-bringer) as well as Daidoukos (torchbearer). Hecate lights the way to the Underworld so that those who descend can do so safely and with less fear. The journey to the Underworld, lit by the light of torches, helps us illuminate the dark parts of ourselves that have remained hidden, perhaps because we have not wanted to look at them. Only when we embrace those parts can we achieve balance between light and dark within our own psyches.

As the goddess of the crossroads, Hecate guides travelers through liminal spaces where roads meet, and they must decide which way to go. In ancient times, crossroads were regarded as magical but often dangerous places, straddling life and death, old and new, familiar and unknown. Hecate was a goddess to call on when faced with a transition—perhaps a move, a new job, a trip, childbirth, marriage, or even death. It was important for those making such transitions to have a goddess they could summon to guide and protect them through such passages. Hecate helped them face such transitions with courage. Images of Hecate were often placed at the entrance to cities or states, in front of homes to ward off evil spirits, or at three-way crossroads. She had the power to let things in as well as keep them out.

Hecate is often depicted as a goddess with three heads looking in the directions of the three-way crossroads; these are usually women's heads, but sometimes they are the heads of a dog, a snake, and a horse. Other depictions show her as three women flanking a column and gazing in different directions. In all these depictions, she sees every route that meets in, or extends from, the crossroads; thus, she is all-wise about the routes for travelers, with a broad perspective that encompasses all possible roads. Some scholars believe that Hecate as a triple goddess represents the fusion of maiden, mother, and crone. As such, she contains all aspects of the feminine divine. She may also symbolize the three phases of the moon, with which she is associated, or past, present, and future.

Hecate is a fearsome figure; some accounts refer to her having snakes for hair: "Hecate of the roads … traverses the sacred crossroads of the land, crowned with oak and the woven coils of snakes falling to her shoulders" (Brannen, 2023). Hecate's crown reflects the two realms she occupies—the Underworld, where snakes live, and the aboveground world of the road, where oak trees grow. She provides a link between the everyday world and the mysterious underworld. Being "of the roads" with her sword, she carries "the force of fighting the powerful who harm others in their quest for glory" (Brannen). She is often invoked for justice for women and children who have been harmed sexually. Like Hecate, many fierce goddesses have this role in protecting women and children and seeking justice for them after sexual harm.

Hecate's two sacred familiars are a black female dog and a polecat, a small animal similar to a ferret or weasel. Both were the products of Hecate's magic. She took mercy on Hekabe, or Hecuba, who murdered a Thracian king after the Trojan War; Hekabe was trying to commit suicide after the murder, but Hecate saved her life by transforming her into the dog who would be her attendant. She also transformed the evil sorceress Gale into a polecat as punishment but then elevated her to the position of her servant. In both cases Hecate took pity on outcasts and made them into sacred figures that served her. Dogs figured centrally in Hecate's myths and worship. They announced her approach with howling. And in rituals, dogs were sacrificed to Hecate and then eaten, a practice we find repugnant today.

Hecate has the reputation of being a "filth eater." In the Greek Magical Papyri, writings from Greco-Roman Egypt describing magical spells and rituals dating from approximately 100 B.C.E., to 400 C.E., she is known as Borborophorba, a figure who eats our garbage after we make the descent into her cave. She recycles our waste, those things that we no longer need and are ready to dispose of. We leave the debris from our lives in her cave and experience healing from letting go of that which no longer serves us. In the safety of her dark womb, we release the traumas and wounds that have kept us stuck. Just as excrement becomes fertilizer for growing plants, our waste becomes life-giving when transmuted by Hecate's magic.

Hecate is known as a psychopomp—a guide to the Underworld after death. Because she and her frequent companion Hermes, also known as Mercury, have the ability to move between worlds, they are natural guides to the afterlife. But Hecate also serves as a midwife, assisting souls who are being born into this world. And her torches help us see the dark parts of ourselves in the shadows of her cave, which we can integrate as newly reclaimed pieces of our souls. Even though Hecate is a fearsome goddess, she stands ready to assist us in the healing process, if we can muster the courage to work with her.

Hecate enables us to break the chains that have held us in the status quo. As such, she was given the title of Rizipyle, or she who frees us from the chains that bind us, in the Greek Magical Papyri texts. She helps us destroy the old ways in order to make room for the new, both in ourselves and the world. She is the ultimate liberator, setting us free from the constraints of social norms and mores that have held us back. She challenges our old modes of thinking that keep us confined to the realm of the ego rather than the expansive world soul.

As children, we may have learned to regard anger as bad, but our journey into Hecate's cave confronts us with all sorts of emotions that we have been taught to regard as unacceptable, including anger. Once we claim our anger, it serves as the fuel to break the chains of social conditioning. We experience a palpable release once we use the energy of our anger to defeat the messages from our past that have kept us in bondage. We become our full, vital, wild selves once we take off our masks of acceptability and conformity. We are free to become our true selves, living in a soulful way. Our righteous anger serves as a healing force that propels us into wholeness. We become sovereign over our own lives, charting our own courses toward self-growth and personal evolution.

As a death queen, or Anassa Eneroi as she is called in the Greek Magical Papyri, Hecate exemplifies the necessary process of undergoing death in order to achieve rebirth. Her cave was a cauldron where transformation from death to rebirth occurred. Her lesson to us is that without death there cannot be new life.

Life, death, and rebirth are all part of the sacred cycles of nature. Hecate, as death queen, does not rule over the Underworld, as does Persephone, Queen of the Underworld (see more about Persephone in the conclusion chapter), but merely guides people to the Underworld and back.

Plato's allegory of the cave in the *Republic* describes a state in which prisoners are chained to a wall, with a fire behind them that casts shadows on a blank wall. Plato contends that the images the prisoners see are not real but simply illusions. For them to see the world as it really is, the prisoners would have to break their chains and ascend from the cave into the light of the sun, which illuminates things as they are. Plato's argument grew out of the patriarchal culture of Greece that put emphasis on light and the sun, typified by male gods.

By contrast, the allegory of Hecate's cave was a product of the matriarchal culture that existed in the Bronze Age (3200-1200 B.C.E.) before matriarchy was overthrown by patriarchy. Plato's description of the cave as a place of darkness that distorts reality is in sharp contrast to the edifying and transformative aspects of Hecate's cave, where people encounter hidden but very real parts of themselves. The chains that imprison people are not found in the cave itself but in the world that rejects the journey into the cave as too treacherous. The story of Hecate's cave is embedded in a matriarchal worldview in which the full knowledge of ourselves is achieved by connecting to a realm that embodies both darkness and light. The fullness of our souls is revealed to us in the darkness of Hecate's cave, illuminated by her torches, not in the blazing sunlight of male gods.

As a guide to the Underworld, Hecate assures us of the new life that awaits us after she purifies us by eating our filth, shines a light on our shadow, and then returns us, transformed, to our everyday world. The journey of descent she offers us enables us to discard the things that have held us prisoner, thus creating the opportunity for liberation into a new order in our lives and in the world.

Tapping into the Dark Goddesses

The dark goddesses exist in the shadow of our psyches. Unless we own them, we can live obliviously in the patriarchal social structure that we were born into, blithely accepting social forces that are like the air we breathe but don't notice because of its invisibility. It is often easier to go along to get along.

When we tap into the dark goddesses in the collective unconscious, we get in touch with a volcanic force that is lying latent, waiting to erupt and change the personal as well as the social landscape. That force has the potential to be revolutionary, overturning a social order that has privileged men and white women. The suppressed rage that lives in the shadows, carried by the dark goddesses, can be a force that reshapes society. The dark goddesses need to emerge from the shadows for the old social order to be destroyed so that a new one can be created—one that brings justice to all members of society, especially those who have been disadvantaged by multiple oppressions. Such a new social structure will benefit everyone—even men, who have also suffered under patriarchy with their own wounds from rigid role expectations. Men, too, have the dark goddesses in their collective unconscious and simply have to look within their shadows to find the liberating power of these goddesses.

CHAPTER THREE

Intersectionality and the Dark Goddesses

> "I am a Black feminist. I mean I recognize that my power as well as my primary oppressions come as a result of my Blackness as well as my womanness, and therefore my struggles on both of these fronts are inseparable."
>
> — Audre Lorde

One of the criticisms often leveled at the feminist movement is that it has primarily been a movement of white women. Black and Brown women exist at the intersection of gender and race, but their experiences in that intersection are not accounted for in the analysis of feminism, which prioritizes gender at the expense of race. Racism has operated to promote white privilege in the feminist movement. White women's experiences are seen as universal, whereas nonwhite experiences are seen as applying only to nonwhite women, who are seen as "other."

The term "intersectionality," coined in 1989 by Kimberlé Crenshaw, a Black feminist legal scholar, has been used to describe the ways in which BIPOC women have been disadvantaged in the fight for women's rights. Only when women of color are included in the feminist movement will it succeed. BIPOC women will lead the way, becoming the tip of the spear.

Criticisms of "white feminism" aptly point out that white feminists have largely ignored the reality of intersectionality and the power differential between white women and women of color. Crenshaw explains that "the intersectional experience is greater than the sum of racism and sexism," noting that "any analysis that does not take that into account cannot sufficiently address the particular manner in which Black women are subordinate" (Crenshaw, 1989).

The history of the women's movement has been fraught with the problem of not recognizing intersectionality, starting with the suffrage movement in the mid-19th century. Suffragists were split on matters of racial equity, with some promoting the rights of women to vote and others the rights of Black people to vote. At the 1866 meeting of the Equal Rights Association, Black author Frances Ellen Watkins Harper implored suffragists "to protect rights for Black Americans and to treat Black women as equals, rather than be 'complicit in … oppression.'" (Griffith, 2022). Elizabeth Cady Stanton removed Harper's comments from the minutes of the meeting. "African American distrust of white reformers was well deserved," according to Griffith. "Its current ran through the history of women's political action, a riptide of racism and white privilege" (Griffith).

The problem of intersectionality is reflected in the film industry, a microcosm of society which exemplifies the larger social issue. *The Hollywood Reporter* notes that over the years, lead actors who are female or from the global majority have fluctuated but are still underrepresented based on U.S. demographics. The Annenberg Inclusion Initiative reports that 41% of leads or co-leads in 2021 were women, who make up 51% of the population, and 32% were people of color, who make up 40% of the population. These relatively high percentages, though not fully proportional to the demographics of these groups, reveal efforts of the film industry to include women and underrepresented racial and ethnic minorities. However, the intersection of these two groups clearly shows where gains still need to be made. Women of color made up just 11% of the leads or co-leads in 2021, a decrease from 17% in 2019. The net result is that for every one female of color in a lead role, there were 2.1 males of color (Neff, 2022).

Women directors are also underrepresented in the film industry. They make up just 21.8% of the field (up from 4.1% in 2011, but still vastly underrepresented). Of women directors, 30.2% were people of color, for a grand total of approximately 7% of all directors who were minority women, a woefully inadequate amount. Of the 76 minority directors in 2021, just 23, or 30%, were women of color, leaving men as 70% of minority directors. These figures show that women are underrepresented in the directing field, but an intersectional analysis reveals that women of color are even more disadvantaged (Neff).

The Academy of Motion Pictures itself is sorely lacking in diversity. A 2023 report by Statista (Statista Research Department, 2023) indicates that 81% of members of the Academy are white and 67% are men, most of whom are older than 60. Numerous actors, including Eddie Murphy, Kim Basinger, and Halle Berry, have complained over the years about the lack of representation of Black people in nominees. In 2015, April Reign created the hashtag #OscarsSoWhite, which went viral, for good reason. Over the 95-year history of the Academy, just 6% of nominees were people of color (1.9% were Black), 17% were women, and only 2% were women of color (Yamata, 2023).

The 2022 film *The Woman King*, a fictional portrayal of the all-female fighting unit of the Dahomey tribe in West Africa, highlights the glaring gaps that remain. The film led box office sales during its first weekend and became one of the highest-grossing films of the year. It received an A+ score from audiences polled by CinemaScore and a 94% Rotten Tomatoes score. An action story that is an alternative to the male-dominated action genre, it features an all-Black, mostly female cast with a Black lead (Viola Davis) and a female director (Gina Prince-Bythewood). If the Academy had been the least bit interested in eliminating the "glaring gaps" in diversity, it would have nominated Davis for best actress and Prince-Bythewood for best director, but the film did not receive a single nomination in any category from the Academy. How can we understand the fact that the film was not just overlooked but actually snubbed by the Academy?

Perhaps it was because the film atypically depicted Black women as powerful, even heroes—roles that are not readily accepted for Black women in our culture. Representing Black women as fighters also defies cultural tropes. And in the film, Davis's character, Nanisca, becomes a woman king, running counter to gender tropes that would at best elevate a woman to the position of queen.

Jessica Chastain, who starred with Davis in the movie *The Help*, spoke out against the snub of *The Woman King* by the Academy. While attending the 48th Chaplin Award Gala in honor of Davis, Chastain said, "When I see a movie like *The Woman King*, it has Viola's fingerprints all over it. A movie like that with a female director and a cast of powerful Black female leads can get made in Hollywood today because of Viola's lifelong advocacy for women of color. Maybe one day a movie like that can get nominated for an Oscar" (Longmire, 2023).

Davis had previously been nominated for best supporting actress for *Doubt* in 2008 and *Fences* in 2016. In both movies she played a "traditional" black woman. In *Doubt* she acted the part of a downtrodden, single mother of a 12-year-old student in a Catholic school in 1964, in an otherwise white student body, who was receiving attention from a priest, leading to suspicion of abuse. And in *Fences*, set in 1950s Pittsburgh, she played a self-sacrificing wife to a domineering and bitter garbage man who lost his chance to play baseball in the majors because he was too old once Black people were permitted to play. Davis received an Oscar for best supporting actress for her performance in *Fences*. In 2020, she was nominated for best actress for her performance in *Ma Rainey's Black Bottom*, about a blues singer in the 1920s who complained that her white bosses valued only her voice, treating her as "just a dog in the alley."

Davis was also nominated for best actress for her 2011 role in *The Help*, in which she played a maid being interviewed by her white employer, who was writing a book about maids. Davis later said that she regretted taking the part, as white voices were centered in the film, leaving out the voices of the Black maids. The movie was criticized for its "white savior" narrative, a cinematic trope in which a white character rescues a person of color from their plight, reinforcing the agency of white people while denying it to people of color. Movie critic Wesley Davis described it as "another Hollywood movie that sees racial progress as the province of white do-gooderism" (Desta, 2018).

All of Davis's roles in movies for which she received a nomination by the Academy reflect the lives of Black women who are oppressed by white society or, in the case of *Fences*, by a patriarchal husband. Her role in *The Woman King*, on the other hand, depicts a powerful woman warrior who is a general in an army of women. It is appalling that the Academy has nominated her for roles in which she has played women marginalized by the intersection of race and gender but snubbed her for a performance that highlights the power a Black woman can have in a gender-nonconforming role. The Academy found it acceptable to nominate her for best actress for her role as a maid but then snub her for her role as a woman warrior. The Academy has a long way to go to eliminate sexism and racism from its picks and overcome its reputation as #OscarsSoWhite.

How can the wisdom of the fierce, or dark, goddesses be brought to bear on the issue of intersectionality? The dark goddesses, most of whom are dark-skinned, integrate intersectionality into the feminist movement. They simultaneously represent the interests of women marginalized by race and gender as well as the interests of all of us, men and women alike. The dark goddesses help us realize that in the feminist fight for a just society, free of patriarchy, women of color will not only be full participants in the struggle but, because they have suffered more from multiple oppressions, they are best positioned to lead an intersectional movement. They have every right to be furious at the marginalized role they have played in the women's movement. And white women have reason, as allies, to be angry at the exclusion of Black, Brown, and Indigenous women, which has splintered the movement.

Kali

One of the most well-known of the dark, or fierce, goddesses, is Kali, a Hindu goddess who is a manifestation of shakti, the primordial energy of the universe, which can be creative as well as destructive. Kali sprang from the forehead of Durga, principal Mother Goddess of Hindu religion, when Durga was besieged by two powerful demons. (Kali's birth from Durga's forehead may be the precursor of the birth of Athena, goddess of war, from the forehead of Zeus, chief father-god in the Greek pantheon.) Kali

Kali

Art by Raja Ravi Varma circa 1900. "Kali Trampling Shiva". Retouched chromolithograph published by Ravi Varma Press. https://commons.wikimedia.org/wiki/File:Kali_by_Raja_Ravi_Varma.jpg

became a source of strength and protection for Durga, destroying the demons to save her life.

Kali, goddess of darkness, destruction, and death, is the quintessential embodiment of shakti, female power. She is a multifaceted icon who expresses many diversified traits. She is pictured stepping on her husband, Shiva, one of the three main male gods in Hinduism, a sign of conquering patriarchy. She signifies the female strength that all women have within them, as well as the fury of women who have been oppressed by patriarchy, both white and nonwhite. Metaphorically, she carries the banner for female liberation. She is the symbol all women need today to inspire them in the fight against patriarchy.

With a scimitar in one hand and the head of a male demon dripping blood in another hand, Kali demonstrates her raw power and victory over patriarchal forces. She sticks out her tongue, showing impudence and impertinence at the social forces that need to be toppled (in much the same way that a child sticks out her tongue in defiance of her parents). Her fierce demeanor speaks to all women, and especially to disenfranchised women who live at the margins of society, who are even more likely to carry rage at multiple oppressions based on gender, race, and class.

Kali is usually depicted as black and sometimes dark blue. She is an archetypal woman of color. As such, she represents both women and people of color in their struggle for justice. As an archetype, she exists in the collective unconscious of women generally, but as a dark goddess, she also represents people of color who lack white privilege. As a universal archetype, she is ready to do battle for all women in their fight for rights. At the same time, she is embedded in the indigenous cultures of South Asia and offers love and protection for the oppressed people who live there. Kali is capable of fighting multiple oppressions simultaneously, transforming systems that oppress on the basis of both gender and race.

A fierce goddess such as Kali has likely arisen in a country such as India, where women have suffered unspeakable abuse, including domestic violence, child marriage, acid throwing, rape, honor killings, dowry killings, and suttee, because she is needed there. "India can arguably be accused of the largest-scale human rights violation on Earth: the persistent degradation of the vast majority of its 650 million girls and women," says Deepa Narayan, social scientist and author of *Chup: Breaking the Silence about India's women* (Narayan, 2018). A 2018 Thompson Reuters Foundation survey ranked India as the most dangerous place in the world to be a woman (Goldsmith, 2018).

Women in India have been worshipping Kali for thousands of years, resonating with her destructive, as well as creative, nature. Kali has provided many women with a model for tapping into their own destructive impulses and acting on them in ways that destroy the old social order to make room for a new, more just, society.

The situation in India is so dire and injustices so pervasive that in recent years, a vigilante group called the Gulaab Gang has sought justice for women when the legal system has failed them. The Gang, composed of half a million women between the ages of 18 and 65, clad in pink saris, fights for the education and safety of women in the Uttar Pradesh province in north-central India. These women warriors seek justice primarily through dialogues, protests, and hunger strikes. When violent crimes against women are committed, the Gang turns perpetrators over to police; but when authorities fail to take action, the gang swoops in with sticks, or rods, thrashing the wrongdoers to teach them a lesson.

Arvind Sen, superintendent of police in the Banda district, has lauded the Gang's work, claiming that "the Gulabi Gang has created such a force of women's rights and awakening that it has brought a new desire to fight against women's exploitation" (Desai, 2014).

While this book does not argue that such "violence" can be condoned, the question of whether such actions are justifiable when the legal system does not protect women remains. For an in-depth discussion of this issue, please see the newly released book *The Furies: Women, Vengeance, and Justice (*Flock, 2024*)*. Leaving aside the question of whether the Gang's actions are justified, the point here is that these women, motivated by their fury, are fighting to restore justice in a system that has denied women equal rights.

Nishita Jain, filmmaker of the documentary *Gulabi Gang*, notes: "It is ironic that in one of India's most backward regions, women are forced to become 'masculine' and aggressive in their fight against machismo and patriarchy" (Desai, 2014). Such claims are often leveled against women who stand up and fight against injustice. Women who are assertive or aggressive are often said to resemble men, abandoning their feminine "virtues" of meekness, accommodation, and people-pleasing. Such sexual stereotyping assumes that women's pugnacity cannot be part of their true nature but must be the result of imitating men. This assumption misconstrues the inherent characteristics of women, depriving them of their own capacity for experiencing righteous anger and rage and acting upon it. Women who refuse to be passive victims are often said to be adopting male characteristics rather than plumbing the depths of their own psyches, owning their own anger at being victimized, and exercising their own agency in creating a society free from such abuses.

The dark goddesses are archetypal representations of Black and Brown people who have been marginalized. By embracing these goddesses and tuning into the powerful rage they carry against oppressive social orders, the feminist movement can create the intersectionality that is sorely needed to wage an effective fight against patriarchy by all segments of society, including those who have suffered with racial inequity.

When white women explore their shadow and own the dark goddesses within, they become allies with Black and Brown women. Such allyship can help overcome the limitations of feminism based on the dominance of white women within the movement. Women of all colors can then join forces to fight the good fight against injustice.

CHAPTER FOUR

Egyptian Dark Goddesses as Archetypes of Women of Color

Isis was "a black and ruddy woman,
endowed with life, sweet of love."
— Inscription at temple of Hathor at Denderah

The Egyptian goddesses Isis and Hathor/Sekhmet are fierce, or dark, goddesses who probably had dark skin. Many historians have speculated that Egyptians were Black, as Sub-Saharan Africans. Ancient Egyptians called Egypt and all of Africa "land of the Black people." Some scholars have even argued that all Black people are descended from ancient Egypt. Michael Jackson's music video "Remember the Time" conveys that premise. The historical Netflix series "Cleopatra" portrays Cleopatra and her courtiers as Black. Many famous Egyptians, such as Queen Nefertari, were depicted with black skin. However, other scholars believe that Egyptians were of Eastern Mediterranean descent, in which case their skin color would have been brown. But in either event, Egyptian dark goddesses have black or brown skin, and as such can also serve as archetypes of women of color in an intersectional analysis.

Isis

ChatGPT AI generated image of Isis statue owned by author.

Isis was the daughter of the sky goddess Nut and the earth god Geb. She was the sister of Osiris, Seth, and Nephthys. Isis and Osiris became wife and husband, as did Nephthys and Seth. Isis was known as the goddess of 10,000 names—the universal and primordial goddess from whom all other gods and goddesses sprang. As such, she is chief among all divinities, encompassing them all and containing both their light and dark aspects. In his second century C.E. book *Golden Ass,* Lucius Apuleius invokes Isis and records her response:

> I am she that is the natural mother of all things, mistress and governess of all the elements, the initial progeny of worlds, chief of the powers divine, queen of all that are in Hell, the principal of them all that dwell in Heaven, manifested alone and under one form of all the gods and goddesses. At my will the planets of the sky, the wholesome winds of the seas, and the lamentable silences of hell be disposed; my name, my divinity is adored throughout the world, in diverse manners, in various customs, and by many names (Gimbutas, 1989).

Isis was a consummate magician who often wielded her magic through trickery. She devised a plot to learn the secret name of Ra, the sun god. The Egyptians believed that names contained a person's essence. If Isis could learn Ra's secret name, she would acquire his magic and surpass his power. One day she noticed that he was drooling in his old age. While he was sleeping, she caught some of his spit and fashioned it into a serpent. (Here Isis's use of the snake as an instrument of power contrasts with the later, Judeo-Christian myth of the snake in the Garden of Eden tempting Eve to eat the forbidden fruit and share it with Adam, which establishes the original sin of humankind at the heart of women's oppression.) The next day Isis placed the snake at Ra's feet, whereupon it bit him with his own poison, the only substance with the power to kill him. Isis convinced him that the only way she could save him was to know his secret name, which he finally surrendered after bluffing with several false ones. Once in possession of the Creator's secret name, Isis usurped his power and became chief Creatrix, with power over all beings and things. After that, she was known as "Great of Magic."

The most popular myth about Isis is one of royal intrigue. Her brother Seth was jealous of Osiris as her consort and coruler of Egypt. Seth used trickery to murder Osiris, throw him into the Nile in a wooden coffin, and usurp the throne.

The mourning Isis searched for her husband's body and found it in Byblos, a seaport in modern Lebanon. His coffin had become part of a tamarisk tree that had been cut down and made into a pillar in the royal palace. Unwilling to leave his body, Isis stayed at the palace and took care of the children there. She became fond of the queen's infant son and decided to use her magic powers to give him eternal life. She cast a spell in which the child was enveloped in fire every evening to burn away his mortal body. The queen happened upon the scene of her burning child and screamed in terror, thus breaking the spell.

Isis became angry at the queen for interfering with her magic, which was designed to give the child immortal life. The queen apologized and asked how she could make reparation to Isis for disrupting her spell. Isis asked for the pillar containing her husband, and the queen agreed. Isis removed the coffin from the pillar and returned to Egypt with it. She hid it in the marshes of the Nile, but Seth found it and, angry at the return of Osiris's body, chopped it into 42 pieces (perhaps corresponding to the 42 provinces of Egypt, although some accounts say 14 pieces). Seth scattered the pieces all across Egypt so they could never be retrieved. With Osiris out of the way, he then ascended to the throne as king.

Isis, in deep mourning for her husband, transformed into a kite, a bird of prey, flying over all of Egypt to retrieve Osiris's body parts. She found them all except the penis, which had been eaten by a fish; she then reassembled the pieces into mummy form. Isis then surrounded Osiris with her wings and breathed life into him. She also used her magic to make Osiris whole again, and with his erect member she conceived a child. At that point Osiris was reborn into the Underworld, with the help of Isis's regenerative magic, and became king of the dead. Nine months later their son Horus was born.

Fearing that Seth would find Horus and kill him, Isis hid Horus in the reeds of the Nile until he was old enough to avenge his father and replace Seth as king. (The story of Isis hiding Horus in the reeds may be the precursor of the story of Moses being hidden in the reeds to protect him from the Pharaoh.) Isis protected Horus from the bites of snakes and scorpions of the Nile delta. The myth does not say exactly how long Horus was hidden, but many statues show Horus as a baby on Isis's lap while she is seated on the throne, clearly indicating that he is the rightful heir. The name "Isis" means "throne," so Horus, sitting on the lap of Isis, is himself sitting on the throne. But the statues depicting Horus on Isis's lap may be strictly symbolic of his future kingship, even if he was still in hiding. Many scholars have noted that such statues likely served as a model for later depictions of baby Jesus on Mary's lap.

There are different accounts of how Seth was eventually defeated in his attempt to usurp the throne from Horus. One story holds that the two transformed into hippopotamuses and fought battles under water for three months. As no victor emerged, the two challenged each other on land. Eventually, as the battle wore on, the gods let Osiris name the victor, who of course was Horus.

The other account of the succession of Horus features Isis as his avenger. The story was recorded in the Papyrus Jumilhac from the second century B.C.E., which had been discovered in Upper Egypt but translated only into French. It was unavailable to English-speaking readers until recently (Forrest, 2020). The story reads that Isis, who magically transformed herself into the warrior goddess Sekhmet, pursued Seth and sent out a flame which destroyed his allies. She positioned herself at an observation point where she could observe Seth, but he transformed into a bull who chased her. In like manner, Isis transformed herself into a hound with a knife attached to its tail and, unrecognizable, chased him. Next, she secured herself in a mountain near Seth and his troops, this time transforming into a cobra. As the troops passed near her, she sank her fangs into them and killed them all with her poison (again here, we see the snake as a symbol of female power in contrast to its later depiction in the Garden of Eden as the agent who brings about female oppression).

In this version of Seth's defeat, Isis reveals herself as a fierce goddess who avenges herself against him with her powerful magic. She does not wait for Horus to defeat Seth but takes on the task herself and single-handedly, rallying her fierce nature to bring about a just conclusion to the struggle between Horus, as the rightful heir to the throne, and the plotting, deceitful Seth. But even in the first version of the story, in which Horus eventually defeats Seth, Isis shows her fierce side by hurling a spear at Seth and cutting off Horus's hands (although she later replaces them magically). In both versions Isis demonstrates her fierceness and puts her insuperable magic to use for a just cause.

Isis typifies the archetype of the dark goddess who possesses a creative as well as a destructive side. She demonstrates her benevolent and magically creative side by bringing her husband back to life after Seth has dismembered him, as well as by creating new life in restoring Osiris's penis and becoming pregnant by him. The fierce side of Isis has often been overlooked or diminished by the various accounts of her story which emphasize her creative side. Her reputation as a "savior goddess" and mother goddess of all the gods has eclipsed her fierce nature, which is highlighted in the Papyrus Jumilhac. With new information from this Papyrus, both sides of Isis's nature as a dark goddess can be balanced and brought into our awareness. She embodied both the life and death aspects of the goddess: "Worshipping Isis was a matter of accepting duality: celebrating life came with honoring death, and vice versa" (Forrest).

Isis is one of the few ancient goddesses who has survived in the hearts of followers and is still worshipped today. The Fellowship of Isis originated in Ireland in 1976 and now exists in 80 countries around the world, with tens of thousands of members. It was acknowledged and represented as a world religion at the Parliament of World Religions, which it also cosponsored, in 1993. Its devotees have created initiatory rites and spiritual practices that honor her. They believe Isis will help to bring about the Aquarian Age as part of her divine plan. The Temple of Isis, a legally recognized church in California that grew out of the Fellowship of Isis in 1996, has priests and priestesses who perform marriages and funerals, pastoral care, baby blessings, and other religious observances. Its humorously stated mission is to provide "catma," not dogma—a feminine perspective that keeps alive the traditions of ancient Egypt as an antidote to pollution, climate change, and violence in today's world. It is not surprising that Isis has endured for more than 2,000 years as a goddess who is still relevant. A supreme deity who cares for the earth and all its creatures with compassion, but also uses her mighty power to fight for a just world, is truly an eternal goddess who has stood the test of time.

Hathor/Sekhmet

Art and image © Lydia Ruyle.

Hathor/Sekhmet

Hathor, an Egyptian Mother Goddess of love, music, dance, and pleasure, is often depicted as a cow or as a woman wearing a cow headdress and a solar disc. Although Hathor has a benevolent, loving side, she also has a destructive side, which manifests as Sekhmet, a woman with the head of a lion, whose name means "Powerful Woman." She is a fierce lioness capable of restoring right order by wiping out the treacherous evildoers.

When the sun god Ra was angry that humanity's agents of chaos were not obeying his rules, which ensured that the cosmic order, known as ma'at, would be preserved, he called upon Hathor to punish them. When she received his entreaty, Hathor transformed into Sekhmet. Hathor's transformation into Sekhmet is reminiscent of Kali springing from Mother Goddess Durga to protect her from evil demons. Such a transformation suggests that fierce rage lies dormant in otherwise benevolent deities and can rise to the surface when needed for protection. The dormant part of the psyche, in the realm of the collective unconscious, is where the dark goddesses live. We can call upon their fierceness, courage, and strength when the just order of the universe is threatened. Sekhmet came into being when the rage inside Hathor was activated.

Sekhmet destroyed the evildoers, as she was called upon to do, but overcome with the taste of human blood, she attacked humankind indiscriminately. Ra knew that he had to intervene to prevent humankind from being wiped out completely. So, he flooded the land with red-colored beer that looked like blood. In her bloodthirsty rampage, Sekhmet lapped it up and became inebriated. She stumbled home in a drunken stupor, and her destruction ceased, at which point she transformed back into Hathor. Ra was happy with this outcome, as his respect among humans had been restored. However, he was so saddened by the pain inflicted on humans by Sekhmet that he decided to leave the world and ascend to the heavens. He climbed onto the back of a cow, possibly Hathor, and was lifted into the sky. His followers, forsaken and left behind, decided to continue his spite of the evildoers on their own. Even though they intended to restore righteousness to the world, they nonetheless introduced murder among humans.

Sekhmet, a bloodthirsty warrior goddess, is a manifestation of female rage as well as the destructive potential of nature. The red beer which Ra poured over the fields, lapped up by Sekhmet, may represent the red silt that covered the land during the inundation of the Nile. The flood of the red waters tempered the parching quality of the sun, which is indicative of Sekhmet's appeasement after her blood feast. As a solar goddess, she is a force of nature in its most destructive form, embodying the burning heat which causes drought but is relieved by the flooding of the Nile. Her nature, like fire, is both destructive and cleansing, burning away that which no longer serves us in order to create a new, and more just, order. Her energy is like a wildfire which destroys forests but leaves the forest floor more fertile with life-giving ash.

Sekhmet was venerated for her destructive power, but like Kali, she had creative as well as destructive aspects. She was greatly feared for bringing death and suffering but also venerated for her healing attributes. She was the patron of healing and fierce protection, able to remove illness and suffering, just as she could mete it out. She needed to be appeased to free people from suffering and restore them to health. She was the cause of disease but also the cure from it—a goddess of contradictions. Egyptians were afraid of her and sought to protect themselves from her as well as to appease and worship her simultaneously.

In her creative aspect, she was known as the Mistress of Life, who could promote life and healing simply by withholding destruction. Devotees could offer her their righteous rage, which can be an act of healing in its own right. Her ferocious nature must always be seen and understood in the context of maintaining order, or ma'at, in the universe, which is fundamentally an act of creation, even if violence is required to achieve it. Sekhmet arose from Hathor when creation was threatened, and her fierce nature is perennially in service to the right order and justice of creation.

CHAPTER FIVE

Virgins

The Black Madonna

> "Whom should I turn to, if not the one whose
> Darkness is darker than night, the only one who keeps
> vigil with no candle and is not afraid—
> The Deep One, whose being I trust…"
> —Rainer Maria Rilke

When Christianity incorporated aspects of earlier cultures' goddesses into its mythology, it modified them to reduce their power and make them less threatening to patriarchy. Christianity, as a patriarchal religion, deprived women of their sexuality, which was seen as sinful but also powerful. Christians held that their god Jesus was not conceived in sin, so his mother, Mary, was, according to doctrine, a virgin. By "virginizing" Mary, the Christian church rendered her less sexual and as such, less threatening to the patriarchy. She was not a full-fledged goddess with intact sexual powers, as was Isis, but a diminished female who took a back seat to her son Jesus. Isis, on the other hand, was an equal to her son Horus, as both were deities. Mary never

Black Madonna

Art and image © Lydia Ruyle.

achieved the status of deity in her own right in the Christian church but was relegated to the mother of the godhead.

While many statues of the Virgin Mary portray her as white, there are a significant number around the world that show her with dark skin, which scholars call Black Madonnas. The Black Madonna's dark skin is a mystery. Some scholars speculate that it may have turned black from the smoke of candles in churches and cathedrals. But most research suggests she was depicted as black intentionally, perhaps because she was thought to have African origins, or because she was an earth goddess with skin the color of rich, dark soil. According to anthropologist and archaeologist Marija Gimbutas, who studied the Neolithic and Bronze Age cultures of "Old Europe," black was the color of earth and life, whereas white was the color of bones and death. For Gimbutas, Black Madonnas illustrated their relationship to the fecund soil; the life-giving quality of the color black was associated with the pre-Christian era.

Jungian scholar Ean Begg says in *The Cult of the Black Virgin* that there are 450 black, brown, or gray Madonnas in the world, not counting ones in Africa. He asserts that "it is indisputable that some of the most famous statues of the Madonna in Western Europe have faces and hands that are black by intention, and are known to have been so for many centuries" (Begg, 1989). Begg speculates that Black Madonnas may be Christianized versions of the pre-Christian goddesses with dark skin who preceded them, such as Isis, Demeter, Cybele, and Artemis. In Italy and Sicily, for example, Black Madonnas are frequently found on sites where temples to the fertility goddesses Ceres and Cybele existed. These ancient goddesses were called upon to ensure a good harvest. Their dark skin was likely related to the dark soil from which the crops grew.

Gilles Quispel, historian of religion at Utrecht University and a student of Jung, was active in researching the Gnostic Gospels, which were found in 1945 in an earthenware jar in Egypt. His studies convinced him that the Black Madonna plays an important psychic role in symbolizing earth, matter, and female sexuality. He wrote that unless people can integrate the primeval image of the Black Madonna, social problems such as racism and misogyny, as well as the conflict between religion and sexuality, will continue (Galland, 1990).

Quispel traces the origin of the Black Madonna to black Artemis at Ephesus, who was venerated in the first millennium B.C.E. in the Temple of Artemis, one of the seven wonders of the world, located on the shores of Asia Minor (now Turkey). Artemis, a Greek goddess of hunting and the wilderness, was the counterpart of the Roman goddess Diana. Although a virgin, Artemis maintained her status as a deity in the prepatriarchal Greek pantheon. She is sometimes depicted as black, perhaps because the original statue in her temple was made from a black meteorite, as referenced in a passage from Acts 19:35 (Bible, n.d.) which referred to Artemis's "image that fell from heaven." Quispel conjectures that the wooden statue of Artemis at Ephesus was painted black to resemble the original statue made from a meteorite.

The citizens of Ephesus were so devoted to Artemis as the Queen of Heaven and Great Mother that after they converted to Christianity, they created a shrine to the only female figure in the new religion, the Virgin Mary, and renamed her Theotokos, Mother of God, in 431 C.E.. Thus, a fusion occurred between the ancient worship of black Artemis and the veneration of Mother Mary as the Black Madonna.

Begg, on the other hand, contends that the Black Madonna was modeled after Isis, who represents the black earth of the Nile.

The priests of Isis wore black, and many of the accoutrements of the Catholic religion, such as incense, holy water, and perpetual lamps, were utilized by worshippers of Isis in the Hellenistic period.

He further illustrates his contention that the ancient origins of the Black Madonna are found in the worship of Isis by pointing to Christian churches built on the sites of Isis temples. For example, the temple of Isis at Soissons, France, was rededicated to the Black Virgin in the fifth century (Begg). Similarly, Santa Sabina, a Christian basilica in Rome, was built over the Temple of Isis in the fourth century, after the Council of Ephesus was convened by Christian bishops.

The oldest Madonna in the world, a brown Virgin in Rome, in the catacomb of Priscilla (wife of a Christian consul), "is considered by some authorities to be Isis," says Begg. In the cathedral of Metz, France, he continues, "a statue of Isis was also venerated as the Virgin until the sixteenth century" (Begg). And the seafaring Apulians introduced the worship of Isis into Lucera, Italy, which Begg claims may have contributed to the eventual prominence of the Black Virgin in that area.

It is generally accepted, he notes, that the images of the Madonna and child in Christian churches had their origin in depictions of Isis holding Horus while seated on a throne. In fact, the name "Isis" is a Greek form of the Egyptian word for throne. Statues of the Madonna and child show Mary seated on a throne, in parallel fashion, with Jesus on her lap. Mary, Begg maintains, inherited the mantle of Isis, although many of the links to her were forgotten or suppressed.

In "Black Madonnas: from Ancient Dark Ancestress to Blessed Virgin Mary," (Rose, 1996) Deborah Rose, who visited sites of the Black Madonna in France, also connects the veneration of Mary to the cult of Isis: "The Romans spread the religion of

Isis throughout their empire and [she] became the supreme deity of the whole Mediterranean world." Rose relates the darkness of the Madonnas to their personification of the material aspect of spirituality, not only in black earth but also in the physicality of their sexuality: "These brown and black madonnas were about being in the body and they held a truer and much older understanding of the sacredness of life on Earth" (Rose).

As noted above, the Christian church denied the sexuality of Mary and the darkness of her body, claiming that she was impregnated without sexual contact, through Immaculate Conception. The result was that the conception of the Mother as tomb as well as womb, embodying fertility and representing the manifestation of spirit that participates in the process of death and regeneration, was lost. In this way the older goddesses lost their power by being stripped of their dark aspects, which represent half their power. Begg concurs that the Black Madonna "has always helped her supplicants to circumvent the rigidities of patriarchal legislation and is traditionally on the side of physical processes—healing the sick, easing the pangs of childbirth, making the milk flow" (Begg). For Rose, our bodies resonate with the Black Madonna, for they remember the past on a collective level: "And the oldest memory is of darkness as the source and the beginning" (Rose).

In *Dark Mother: African Origins and Godmothers*, Lucia Chiavola Birnbaum traces the spread of Black Madonnas throughout Europe to the migration of Africans who brought Isis with them: "Images of black madonnas may be our most palpable evidence of the persisting memory of the primordial dark mother of Africa on the continent of Europe" (Birnbaum, 2001). She explains the diffusion of African Isis into Europe by identifying ancient migration routes from Africa. For instance, the Black Madonna at Brucoli, Sicily, known as Madonna dell'Adonai, is on such a route. Africans who migrated there left the color black on their image of the Mother, painted on a grotto wall. There are so many Black Madonnas in France, she says, because southern France was on the paleolithic migration and sailing route from Africa. But for Birnbaum, the Black Madonna has become a universal figure, the African mother of us all whose influence is found in cultures throughout the world. Rose echoes Birnbaum's sentiment: "The dark mother is the original mother" (Birnbaum).

The Black Madonna has become the symbol of political liberation and justice for the oppressed masses. For example, the Black Madonna, known as Our Lady of Czestochowa, has come to represent the independence and identity of Poland. All the victories of Poland over attacks or invasions have been attributed to her intercession. Known as the Queen of Poland, she has become the symbol of the antiauthoritarian Solidarity movement, which has been subject to government repression. Its leader, Lech Walesa, always wore a medallion of the Black Madonna of Czestochowa on his lapel, and he dedicated his Nobel Peace Prize to her.

Interestingly, the face of Our Lady of Czestochowa has scars that are suggestive of scarification rituals in Africa. The Black Madonna may represent not just the dark feminine which lives in the collective unconscious but also a mother figure that has its historical and psychological roots in Africa. No one really knows how the scars on the Black Madonna's face got there. My hunch is that they trace back to her origins in Africa, where scarification rituals were performed.

One of the most famous Black Madonnas was found in Chartres Cathedral in France. Known as Notre Dame de Pilar, a 1508 dark wooden copy of a silver- and gold-plated Madonna from the 13th century, she was painted white in 2013 during the renovation of the Cathedral. The transformation of the Black

Madonna to a white Madonna was severely criticized for wiping out a cultural memory that had persisted for 500 years. A plaque under the figure reads that the "unsightly coating" had been removed. Another Black Madonna, Notre Dame de Sous-Terre, an 1857 replica of the original that burned during the French revolution, still survives in a crypt in the Cathedral.

Jungian analyst Fred Gustafson found that Black Madonna archetypes appeared in dreams reported by his patients. He concludes that these Madonnas are symbolic of "femininity that is dark and acts as the matrix of all creativity and renewal" (Gustafson, 1990). He writes that the blackness relates to the fact that the feminine is seen as inferior in patriarchal religions, which honor reason and intellect above the deep mysteries of the soul, more aptly pictured as black. Worshippers of Black Madonnas, he says, resonate with their soulful quality, which he calls the Dark Feminine. Nonpatriarchal religion or spirituality is often seen as less masculine and more emotional or feminine. Gustafson sees the Black Madonna as a manifestation of Jung's mother archetype, a universal figure that exists "in every person and every culture" (Gustafson). An inscription on the altar of a cathedral in Salerno, Italy, supports Gustafson's view: "Darkness preceded light and She is Mother."

Robert Graves, in *The White Goddess,* makes a similar point in tracing the origin of Black Madonnas in France and Sicily to the ancient tradition of wisdom as black (Graves, 1948).

He claims that Black Virgins, harking from this tradition, represent nonpatriarchal relationships between the sexes—"a new pacific bond between men and women." Begg agrees that the Black Madonna was retained as a powerful but solitary female figure in a patriarchal religion which devalued women and nature; as such, she stands for the healing power of nature and loving, nonhierarchical relationships between men and women.

"Our ancient, battered, much-loved, little-understood Black Virgins are a still-living archetypal image that lies at the heart of our civilization and has a message for us," Begg maintains. "The feminine principle is not a theory but real and it has a will of its own which we ignore at our peril" (Begg). Now that the Black Virgins have been rediscovered with their ancient wisdom, he says, they carry a charge from the goddess which we must heed, as the future of civilization depends on it.

Lilith

Art and image © Lydia Ruyle.

CHAPTER SIX

Demons

"Adam's First Wife Lilith: Diabolical Demoness
or the First Feminist?"
—Rabbi Allen Maller

Lilith

In addition to virginizing ancient goddesses, the Judaeo-Christian tradition also demonized them. Under patriarchy, there were only two options for women—virgin or demonic whore. In ancient Sumerian myths, which became the basis for the Torah and Old Testament writings, Lilith was the first woman. She was Adam's first wife, but she refused the lie beneath him as subordinate during sex and so is sometimes considered the first feminist.

The creation story of the Zohar, a text that provides the foundation of mystical writings of the Jewish Kabbalah, reads that Lilith and Adam were created at the same time out of earth by God. They were part of an androgynous whole, with two faces looking in opposite directions. God sawed them in two, thus creating Lilith: "Now in the depth of the great abyss there is a certain hot fiery female spirit named Lilith, who at first cohabited with man" (Koltuv 1986). Adam and Lilith were equal because they both originated from soil to which God gave form; it was also the reason Lilith gave Adam for her equality and for her justification in not bending to Adam's demand that she lie underneath him during sex.

The creation story in Genesis of the Christian Bible (which includes the Old Testament) does not, however, mention Lilith. It starts with God saying he would create a helper for Adam: "It is not good that the man should be alone; I will make him a help meet for him. … And the Lord God caused a deep sleep to fall upon Adam, and he slept: and he took one of his ribs and closed up the flesh … and [from] the rib, which the Lord God had taken from man, he made a woman and brought her unto the man" (Holy Bible, n.d., Genesis 2:18-21). The woman, whom Adam later named Eve, was thus created from the body of Adam. She was not created as the equal of Adam, as was Lilith, who became a separate being when the original androgyne was cut into two equal parts. Instead, Eve was derived from the flesh and bone of Adam and was designed to be his helpmate, not his equal.

Lilith was never a helpmate, as she sought a relationship with Adam that preserved her freedom and equality. She was unwilling to bow to patriarchal authority during sex. When Adam didn't accept her refusal to submit to him sexually, she uttered the ineffable name of God, which was prohibited in Jewish tradition, and fled to the desert wilderness by the Red Sea. Like Isis, she knew the secret name of God, which speaks to the sacred power she possessed.

Such power indicates that she was a force to be reckoned with, perhaps as a goddess in her own right. In fact, according to Raphael Patai, "Lilith had to become God's Hebrew Goddess consort in order to learn and use the unspoken name to escape Adam" (Patai, 1990). Lilith was God's equal, or at least on intimate terms with him, and used her sacred power to resist domination by Adam. Lilith used whatever means were necessary to escape Adam and his patriarchal demands. Her utterance of God's sacred name suggests her superiority to Adam in matters of divine knowledge, which gives justification for her unwillingness to bend to his authority. But since speaking God's name was forbidden, it may also have been an act of rebellion against Adam and the patriarchal structures he represents. Or it may simply have been used in Jewish scriptures as another reason to demonize her.

In Jewish folklore, Lilith was known as a night demon, or succubus, who visited men in their dreams, causing them nocturnal emissions. She was the original femme fatale whose blatant sexuality tempted men. After leaving the Garden of Eden, she engaged in fornication with men as they slept. God commanded her to return to the Garden, but she refused. Her punishment was that 100 of her children would die each day. She herself became a baby killer, perhaps as revenge for having her own children killed.

Her nature as a wild, untamed creature is apparent in the desolate wilderness she flees to after leaving the Garden: "Wild cats will meet hyenas there; the satyrs will call to each other; there Lilith shall repose and find her a place of rest" (Jewish Publication Society Bible, n.d. Isaiah 34:14). In Gematria, a Kabbalistic practice of assigning numbers to names, Lilith's name means "screech," which led to her being called a screech owl. In a Sumerian terracotta relief, circa 2000 B.C.E., she is depicted as "Queen of the Night" with wings and owl feet, surrounded by her familiars—two owls, symbolizing wisdom—while standing on the backs of two lions, which may symbolize her dominion over animals associated with masculine authority or kingship. In her hands she holds rods with rings, sacred symbols which identify her as a goddess, not the demon she is purported to be. On her head she wears a headdress adorned with several rows of horns, another symbol of a goddess.

Lilith is most likely Black, as the Sumerians called themselves black-headed people. However, the Sumerians lived in the southern part of the modern state of Iraq, so they may have been Brown like current residents of Arab descent. Lilith, a dark goddess, is a woman of color, either Black or Brown; as such she represents women of color who use their power to resist patriarchal oppression.

How is it possible to reconcile the depiction of Lilith as a wise goddess with her reputation as a seductive demon? Since she knew the creator's name, gained through intimacy with him, she may have been the original goddess to the god. Her potent sexuality would have been a revered attribute of ancient, life-giving mother goddesses that were worshipped in the Neolithic civilization of the goddess. But she refused to have her sexuality controlled by Adam, which was seen by Jewish scholars as an act of disobedience against patriarchal authority. Her powerful nature, perceived as a threat to the patriarchy, was demonized. Her story was a lesson to women to submit to domination by men or be labeled as evil demons, harlots, or baby killers.

Patriarchy needs to control women's sexuality, as is evident today in women's reproductive rights being stripped and women being shamed and criminalized for "killing" their babies by having abortions. During the so-called Renaissance, witches too were in touch with the earth and its useful herbs, their own sexuality, and the need to help deliver babies. They paid a serious price for their life-enhancing, life-sustaining ways; we can't forget how they were demonized and burned at the stake.

Lilith was a free spirit who chose to live alone in the wilderness rather than submit to Adam's authority. Her wings, like those of ancient bird goddesses, carried her to freedom.

Women today need to find their wings to escape the tyranny of patriarchy. We cannot fly to a remote desert, but we can reclaim our wild nature, which connects us to earth with all its wild creatures—the earth from which both Adam and Lilith were created, the original source from which we all sprang, not from Adam's rib.

Lilith was demonized because she acted up and asserted herself, refusing to be the quiet, passive, docile helpmate that Eve was created to be. These two sisters are prototypes of the either-or roles that have been prescribed for women under patriarchy—either saint or prostitute. Women have been subjugated as Eves ever since patriarchal cultures, brought to Old Europe by invaders of Indo-European descent from the steppes of Russia, overtook ancient matriarchal cultures, which valued partnership and equality between the sexes.

Lilith has become a role model for women who refuse to be dictated to and who take ownership of their sexuality as their birthright. Lilith won because she achieved freedom from unjust authority. Women today need to fight for their freedom just as Lilith did, but they risk the fate that Lilith met with, living alone and demonized as evil and predatory. However, the catch is that even women who mold themselves to be like Eve, compliant and passive, yielding to domination by men, end up being perceived as evil too. Eve was blamed for tempting Adam to eat from the fruit of the tree of knowledge and bore the guilt for that ever after. She was banished from the Garden and punished by God with severe pain during childbirth, while remaining under Adam's rule.

In patriarchal culture, women cannot win either way. They carry the guilt of humankind and cannot escape being labeled as sinful, whether they abide by patriarchal rules or not. This is the dilemma women have faced for millennia. They are considered evil just for being women. Their nature makes them inherently bad—responsible either for the fall from grace, as Eve, or for haunting men at night as succubi, as Lilith; succubi need men's semen to survive, a reversal of roles in which men become the life-givers rather than women. How can women heal this split between the two sides of women portrayed in the Bible, and how can they come into their own without carrying guilt and blame for evil in the world?

The dualism of Western civilization has split the world into good and evil, light and dark, and has projected evil and darkness onto women because of their sexuality. The only female who can be seen as good is a virginal figure like Mary, who was impregnated by the holy spirit, not through sexual intercourse. Christian theology vilified female sexuality, with the resultant split between saint and whore, while Jewish teachings reserved goodness only for the Shekinah, a disembodied feminine principle that is the source of light and wisdom. Sexuality was considered dangerous, as even God, in Jewish literature, succumbed to temptation by Lilith and made her his consort; she was wily in using her sexuality to learn God's name. In both Christianity and Judaism, women are seen as the source of evil and must be punished for their inherent guilt. Hence in Western culture, man became good and woman bad. Female sexuality was the root of all evil and must be controlled by men, a theme playing out today in political restrictions placed on women's bodies, primarily by white men (who of course believe they are in God's image and that their actions are thus sanctified by him).

Neolithic cultures, by contrast, envisaged a goddess who contained all dualities within herself—good and evil, life and death, light and dark. Female sexuality was affirmed and revered as the source of life. Temples to the goddess, such as the temple of Aphrodite in Corinth, Greece, and the temple of Inanna in

Sumeria, often had sacred prostitutes whose bodies became the means of communing with the goddess and the life force she represented. At the same time, the goddess wielded the power of death, deciding when lives must end, plunged into her cauldron of death and rebirth. The powers of life, death, and regeneration were all contained within her, just as they were found in nature, whose powers she encompassed.

Ancient goddess cultures saw the world as both good and evil, existing together in a unified whole, each containing the essence of the other. The universe was not perceived as morally black and white, where the forces of good and evil combat each other; instead, good and evil were seen as inextricably connected, part of the forces and cycles of nature that were in harmony with each other, in a worldview that saw the universe as essentially amoral. Nature, like the goddess, is both creative and destructive, to be accepted in all its aspects.

Lilith represents the dark and feminine aspect of divinity that has been split off from the whole and demonized. The theological underpinnings of Western culture have led us to see the divine as limited to the good rather than encompassing both good and evil. The primal female energy personified by Lilith, including her unabashed sexuality, has been maligned and excluded from our understanding of the sacred. As women, we need to acknowledge that Lilith is part of the dark, or shadow side, of our psyches and reclaim our sexuality as sacred. She is the archetypal witch, identified by Jung, who lives in our collective unconscious. We must excavate her from our depths and give her new life. Only then will we be free and whole.

CHAPTER SEVEN

Reproductive Rights

"A woman's right to choose an abortion is something central to a woman's life, to her dignity. … And when government controls that decision for her, she's being treated as less than a full adult human being responsible for her own choices."
—Ruth Bader Ginsburg

We are living in a society that has come out of repressing and demonizing the wholeness of the fierce goddesses and thus women in general. Abortion is the issue where we see women's rights coming into conflict with patriarchy most starkly, as patriarchal oppression is most evident in striking women's reproductive rights. The Supreme Court decided to overturn Roe v. Wade, the case which gave American women the right to abortion in 1973, in the case of Dobbs v. Jackson Women's Health Organization in June 2022. This decision dealt a blow to one of the most basic freedoms of women—control over their own bodies. Now that abortion access is left to the states, no longer federally protected, the health of pregnant women will be negatively impacted in many states. We need to remember the landscape that existed before Roe took effect. It is what life (or death) will look like for American women if the antiabortion movement has its way.

Before Roe v. Wade, back-alley abortions were common, but many women used whatever means were necessary to terminate their own pregnancies—coat hangers, knitting needles, sticks, ballpoint pens, even chicken bones. Others ingested turpentine, acid, or bleach. Some were successful, but many bled to death or died of infection. All major hospitals had septic abortion wards for women who nearly died while trying to abort their pregnancies. Some women injured or killed themselves by jumping off roofs or throwing themselves down stairs in attempts to abort. Low-income and BIPOC women suffered the most, as they didn't have the means to obtain clandestine abortions from private doctors or travel to foreign countries.

The Supreme Court is now inflicting its right-wing views on a country that does not share its values; most Americans support a woman's right to abortion (Pew Research Center, 2024). "The triumphal right," said Susan Faludi in an interview with Michelle Goldberg, "has taken the gloves off and is pursuing a scorched-earth campaign against women's most fundamental rights. No more faux hand-wringing about saving women from spinsterhood or 'post-abortion syndrome.' This is just 'Lock her up!'" (Goldberg, 2022). Just as Lilith and other powerful goddesses were demonized for their sexual freedoms, women today who have abortions are demonized as loose women and baby killers.

The Dobbs decision set the stage for rights other than abortion to be stripped as well, including rights protecting birth control, same-sex consensual relationships, and same-sex marriage, all of which fall under the due process clause of the Fifth and 14th Amendments, which recognized the right to privacy. Supreme Court Justice Clarence Thomas, in a sole concurring opinion overturning Roe v. Wade, called for all three rights to be reconsidered. Lesbian couples may be especially impacted by reproductive rights being abridged—first by being unable to marry and second by having limited options to have children if in vitro fertilization is restricted.

Rights to contraceptives may also be off the table because of their alleged potential to destroy a human life; the morning-after pill and IUDs, erroneously considered abortifacients, are especially under attack. Currently, the right to contraception is protected by two Supreme Court decisions: Griswold v. Connecticut (1965) and Eisenstadt v. Baird (1972). The due process clause of the 14th Amendment formed the basis of the right to engage in same-sex, consensual-sexual activity in private, as decided in a 2003 case by the Supreme Court, but that precedent can be challenged and overturned. And same-sex marriage may also be in jeopardy if it is no longer considered protected by the due process clause. The Respect for Marriage Act, passed in December 2022, requires that all states recognize same-sex marriage performed in states where it is legal and grants federal recognition of such marriages. However, the legality of same-sex marriage still rests on the 2015 Supreme Court decision in Obergefell v. Hodges, which recognized same-sex marriage as constitutionally protected by the due process clause. The Supreme Court could overturn Obergefell, just as it did with Roe, and thereby outlaw same-sex marriage.

There may also be restrictions on the genetic testing, storage, and disposal of embryos created by IVF. There are four main situations in which procedures related to IVF may be impacted by Dobbs: discard of unused embryos; freezing of embryos for later use; genetic testing of embryos to rule out fetal abnormalities; and reduction of the number of fetuses in utero to ensure the survival of the remaining ones. So far, the courts have not ruled on any of these situations post Dobbs, but it is possible they will do so in the future.

The personhood of fetuses from the moment of conception is making its way into discussions of the abortion issue in state legislatures and is the new frontier in arguments about the legality of abortion. Arizona passed a personhood bill in 2021, but federal Judge Douglas Rayes blocked the bill in 2022. If embryos and fetuses are legally considered persons, pregnant women may be eligible for child support payments from fertilization onward. If fetal personhood is made legal in some states but not others, it will be confusing to have no federal standard about what constitutes a human being with all the attendant rights.

Another issue that is being hotly debated is the access to medication-induced abortion. Most abortions in the U.S. occur with medication, not surgery. A combination of mifepristone and misoprostol enables women to have abortions in the safety and privacy of their own homes. The Supreme Court has agreed to decide whether access to mifepristone can be limited. Even if the Court rules against mifepristone, misoprostol can be used alone to end pregnancies, although it causes more cramping and bleeding. In the meantime, mifepristone remains available in states where it is legal.

In 2023, Judge Matthew Kacsmaryk, a U.S district judge in Texas who was appointed by Donald Trump, cited the Comstock Act of 1873 in prohibiting the mailing of abortion pills in a case brought by the Alliance for Hippocratic Medicine, an antiabortion group. The Act, which has since had many of its provisions overturned, makes it illegal to send "obscene" material through the mail, including anything used to induce an abortion. Later court rulings held that the Act applies only if senders of such materials intend them to be used illegally. Since abortion was legal during Roe, the Act did not apply, but now that Roe has been overturned, abortion opponents are trying to use this antiquated law to outlaw sending abortion medications through the mail. Stay tuned.

The Supreme Court, whose justices masquerade as impartial interpreters of the law, has not acknowledged the religious ideology driving its decision. All five of the majority grew up in the Catholic Church, which holds that abortion is wrong because life begins at conception and must be protected from that point forward. The majority justices were appointed by conservative presidents who wished to stack the court in favor of antiabortion views. President Trump handpicked Amy Coney Barrett, well-known for her opposition to abortion, to overturn Roe v. Wade; he then bragged that he killed Roe.

The Dobbs decision focuses almost entirely on the protection of unborn fetuses, neglecting to give meaningful attention to the experience and rights of women carrying such fetuses. The Court saw fit to ignore the doctrine of *stare decisis* (the doctrine of adhering to legal precedent) and overturn a precedent that had stood for 50 years. What could have been so significant that it led the justices to overturn a well-established right to abortion, if not their own religious beliefs? Injecting such unacknowledged beliefs into decisions violates the separation of church and state, upon which our country was founded. The antiabortion movement in the U.S. has emerged from a strongly misogynist Christian theology which imposes its views on everyone.

Judaism, by contrast, prioritizes the life and health of the mother over the potential life of the fetus. For Jews, human life does not begin at conception but rather when the fetus' head or the majority of its body leaves the mother's body. Until that time, the fetus is considered part of the mother's body and cannot be given priority because it is not yet deemed to have an independent existence. Abortion is thus permissible at every stage of pregnancy if the fetus poses a risk to the life of the mother. The Dobbs case invalidates Jewish beliefs about abortion and imposes Christian theology on Jews, whose religious beliefs are not protected—a clear violation of the separation of church and state. "If we're going to live in a religiously free society," says Rabbi Daniel Bogard of the Central Reform Congregation of St. Louis, "we are each allowed to interpret ... on our own for our own tradition, and a minority in this country can't impose their conservative white Christian religiosity on the rest of us." He adds that he expects a wave of lawsuits based on religious freedom (Figueroa, 2022).

The theocratic underpinnings of the Dobbs decision are reminiscent of Margaret Atwood's 1985 book *The Handmaid's Tale* about a theocracy in which women in the "handmaid" class are forced to become impregnated and give birth. The book has been described as prophetic of the theocratic leanings of the American political system which have ultimately led to the Dobbs decision as well as other religiously based Supreme Court decisions.[3]

Some pro-choice advocates argue that abortion is not a moral issue but rather a medical issue best left to a woman and her doctor to decide. It can be argued that even if it is a moral issue, that does not mean that it is within the province of the legal system to regulate. There are numerous examples of moral issues that are left to the individual to decide rather than legally regulated. Examples include eating animals, lying, and failing to provide aid or intervene when another person is in a life-threatening situation; the Kitty Genovese case, where bystanders did not even call the police while witnessing a homicide, is a

[3] A case in point is the football coach who prayed on the field after games. The case was upheld by the 6-3 majority of conservatives on the bench.

good example of the last (Gansberg, 1964). Many cases in which moral issues are left to the individual to decide are considered outside the scope of the law; often these are said to fall under the right to privacy, protected by the 14th Amendment, as abortion was prior to the Dobbs decision.

A legal system overreaches when it injects religious or moral views into the law. The law then operates as the "morality police," as it has, for example, with same-sex consensual relationships, which were previously outlawed by sodomy laws on the grounds that such relations were immoral. Such laws were derived from church law, which found that nonprocreative sex was immoral. And although sodomy laws were overturned in 2003 in Lawrence v. Texas, the religious leanings of the current Supreme Court may in fact overturn that case, as Justice Thomas has suggested it might very well do, if the Court holds that 14th Amendment no longer protects it.

Twenty-one states ban most abortions as of this writing. Already children as young as 10 who are victims of rape or incest have been forced to give birth, often jeopardizing their health as well as their lives and depriving them of the ability to chart the course of their own futures. A 10-year-old's body is not meant to carry and deliver a child. A child's hips don't enlarge until late adolescence (Pappas, 2012), and rates of eclampsia, infection, and postpartum endometritis are higher (Ganchimeg et al., 2014). Being a victim of rape or incest is traumatic, and being forced to deliver a child adds more trauma. When traumatized children must parent children, the psychological effects on both are likely to be disastrous. A mental health system that is already taxed stands to be strained even more.

With states now free to regulate abortion without federal interference, the issue in many cases has become not just whether women can have legal abortions but whether they or their providers will face criminal charges and prison time. The same is true of women who accidentally harm their fetuses (e.g., by not wearing a seat belt during a car accident or delaying a C-section) or "chemically endangering" them by using drugs, even prescribed medications. And today women taking antiaddiction medicine to wean off opioids are being punished by having their children taken away (Walter, 2023). Even in states where exceptions for the life or health of the mother are allowed, doctors are often unwilling to perform abortions in such cases for fear of prosecution. And women who miscarry may not receive the medical care they need because doctors fear they will be charged with assisting an abortion.

Like Lilith, women today are being demonized and punished for their sexuality by the Christian theology that influences our judicial system at the highest levels. In the push to restrict women's reproductive freedoms, we see the continued repression of the power of the fierce goddesses over both creation and destruction.

Nana Buruku

As a protector of women in their reproductive capacity, the West African goddess Nana Buruku is the goddess women can look to for protecting their reproductive rights. Nana Buruku is a strong West African goddess whose name means "wicked grandmother." Also known as Nana Bouclou and Nana Buluku, she is worshipped in Nigeria, Ghana, Togo, and Benin. She is often depicted as a crone who guides women, especially mothers and women seeking help with fertility. She is a fierce goddess who can be appealed to by pregnant women in need of protection as well as women seeking abortions. She presides over the life-giving potential of women as well as the destructive power they have to terminate pregnancy. She has, for instance, the power to

Nanã Buruku or Nana Buluku an Orisha of Candomblé.
https://commons.wikimedia.org/wiki/File:Nana_Buruku.jpg. CCA-SA 2.5 license (https://creativecommons.org/licenses/by-sa/2.5/deed.en).

destroy a pregnancy if it occurs through unjust means such as rape. Symbolically, she stands for the power women rightfully have over their own bodies.

Nana Buruku's color is lavender/purple, and ritual necklaces for her are lavender and white or black. She is frequently depicted with jewelry made of cowrie shells (a symbol of female genitalia) and a veil made of beads. Her magical number is seven, which may refer to the seven chakras; worshippers may call on her when they feel their energy system is out of balance, although they may suffer discipline or punishment if they don't follow her guidance. Her followers believe she embodies the spirit of the African baobab tree, a symbol of strength and longevity, and she is often pictured wearing leaves from the tree. She carries a hook-shaped spiritual broom, a symbol of purification and cleansing which she uses to guide those seeking spiritual transformation.

Nana Buruku's fierce power is illustrated in her conflict with Ogun, a warrior god who rules over metallurgy. She was in the forest taking in the sights and smells of the animals when Ogun entered with his machete, planning to hunt animals. Most of them fled except for a deer, which Ogun pursued with his blade. Nana Buruku intervened, shape-shifting into a giant snake[4] which incited terror in him and caused him to flee. The deer, grateful that Nana Buruku had saved its life, imbued her with the right to receive sacrifices of deer. But any such sacrifices must be made with wood or bamboo knives, which have become tools that honor her and her power over Ogun.

Nana Buruku came to the New World with West Africans in slave ships, who were put to work on sugarcane, tobacco, and cotton plantations. As a result, she is also venerated in Voodoo-

[4] Much like in the myth of Isis, here the snake is a symbol of power rather than original sin, as it is in Genesis.

based religions in Louisiana; the French, Dutch, and British West Indies; and Brazilian Candomblé. In Hoodoo, a spiritual tradition in the southern U.S. which is a syncretic version of Voodoo, Christianity, and local herbalism, Nana Buruku is associated with St. Anne, mother of Mary and grandmother of Jesus. Her powers are not limited to these cultures, however, as women anywhere can call on her. Nana Buruku is needed now more than ever to protect and defend women's reproductive rights in the midst of a backlash which threatens to eradicate them.

CHAPTER EIGHT

Women's Health and Safety Are Feminist Issues

"He is the Subject, he is the Absolute—she is the Other."
— Simone de Beauvoir

Men as the Default

The denial of women's bodily autonomy that we see most starkly in the fight to deny women the right to abortion is perhaps the most visible aspect of Western culture's conception of women's bodies as inferior to men's, but the harm this paradigm causes women extends much further. Women's rights generally have paled beside those of men for centuries. For example, the right to quality, comprehensive health care for women has never been fulfilled, as equitable health care has not been given priority by the medical system.

The ancient Greek philosopher Aristotle set the groundwork for our Western culture's view of women. Aristotle espoused the idea that women are merely mutilated men, which has influenced how they are treated by the medical system. Aristotle described women as immature, deficient, and even monstrous, as he thought they failed to develop into the perfection of manhood. Women were, he claimed, men turned outside in, with ovaries as female testicles and the uterus as scrotum. The reason these parts of female anatomy were not external was because women lacked the "vital heat" to convert them. Another Greek philosopher, Pythagoras, said man is the measure of all things. He was making a point about truth, but his androcentrism bleeds through, as "man" is considered to be gender-neutral, while "woman" is seen as gender-specific.

Seeing man as the default has had devastating health consequences for women. As a case in point, heart disease is the leading cause of death in U.S. women (Office on Women's Health, 2023). And women are more likely to die from heart attacks than men. Despite these numbers, doctors are likely to overlook heart disease in women, as their medical training has focused on cardiovascular disease in men.

Physicians often miss a diagnosis of heart disease because it presents differently in men and women. Women are less likely to have chest and arm pain (a common presentation in men) and more likely to have stomach pain, breathlessness, nausea, and fatigue, often considered atypical (Perez, 2021). Heart attacks are usually diagnosed with angiograms, which look for obstructed arteries, which women frequently lack, resulting in women being sent home with a diagnosis of nonspecific chest pain and told they do not have heart disease.

But in cases where women are actually diagnosed with heart failure and need an artificial heart, their chests are often too small to accommodate the heart, which has been designed for men. Shockingly, the designers of the artificial heart did not even consider whether they would fit in women's bodies (Perez). The heart is now undergoing redesign, but only after the "oops" of discovering it didn't fit in many women.

Women's Pain Ignored

Women are less likely than men to be believed by doctors when they say they have pain. Often women's complaints are ignored, and treatment is neglected. In many instances doctors label them as crazy or prescribe tranquilizers and antidepressants. A recent podcast by the *New York Times*, "The Retrievals," describes cases that occurred at the Yale Fertility Center (Burton, 2023). Women who underwent egg retrieval for IVF complained of excruciating pain during the procedure, in which a needle is inserted through the vaginal wall into the ovary. They were given pain medication, which didn't seem to work. Some said they felt everything. Others screamed and expressed doubt about whether they could complete the procedure. For months the clinic dismissed their complaints. The staff came to assume that women would experience pain during the procedure, even with medication. One woman who complained of torturous pain was told she had received the maximum dose of pain medicine. And so the retrievals continued.

Eventually it was discovered that a nurse who worked at the clinic had stolen the pain medication, fentanyl, to support her addiction and replaced it with saline solution. But in the meantime, many women had suffered needlessly, and some did not return to the clinic for additional retrievals, which robbed them of their chance to have a child. It's impossible to know how many avoided other procedures, such as biopsies or IUD insertions, for fear of pain. But the trauma the women experienced had lasting effects and eroded their trust in the medical system. "The Retrievals" brought attention to an egregious case in which women's pain was ignored, but the problem of dismissing women's pain is widespread and persists in varying degrees throughout the medical establishment.

Often women have pain syndromes related to diseases they have more commonly, such as migraines and irritable bowel syndrome, or sex-specific maladies such as menstrual cramps (Perez). Doctors tend to overlook pain in such cases. And even when they do prescribe painkillers, they tend to wait longer in prescribing them to women. For instance, in the case of acute abdominal pain in U.S. emergency rooms, women wait an average of 65 minutes before receiving painkillers while men wait only 49 minutes (Harvard Health Blog, 2017). To make matters worse, there is evidence that women are more sensitive to pain than men (Perez), making the failure to treat them for pain even more egregious.

The Menopause Malady

In addition to ignoring women's pain, the medical system does not give adequate attention to women's suffering in general, with menopause being an example. Psychiatrist Rebecca Thurston, who studies menopause at the University of Pittsburgh, believes that menopausal women are underserved. "It suggests that we have a high cultural tolerance for women's suffering. It's not regarded as important," she says (Dominus, 2023). Symptoms vary but include hot flashes, sleeplessness, mood swings, irritability, problems concentrating, memory problems, headache, vaginal dryness, painful sex, accelerated bone loss, joint pain, weight gain, low libido, increased risk of heart disease, and heavy periods (the last during perimenopause, the period leading up to the cessation of menses). If men had these symptoms, would medicine turn a blind eye to them? Would doctors be content to reassure them that the process was natural? Your guess is as good as mine.

Women who experience such symptoms are often overlooked despite the fact that there is good treatment—hormone replacement therapy, which has been around since the 1960s. In 1991, Bernadine Healy, the first woman director of the National Institutes of Health, launched the Women's Health Initiative, a randomized clinical trial of hormone treatment of postmenopausal women. The study was expected to run 15 years but was brought to a halt in 2002, when it was announced that the risks of hormone therapy (heart disease, strokes, clots, and breast cancer) were greater than the benefits. An interview on the *Today* show with Sylvia Wassertheil-Smoller, chief investigator for the Women's Health Initiative (W.H.I.), caused panic among women taking hormones.

Although the risks of HRT were accurately reported, they were not put in context. For instance, the increased risk of breast cancer was 26%, but that meant increasing the risk from 2.33% to 2.94%, a small incremental risk. After the interview on the *Today* show, insurance claims for HRT dropped dramatically—by 30% in six months and by 70% in seven years. Dr. JoAnn Manson of Brigham and Women's Hospital and one of the investigators of the study, said the sudden drop in use of HRT created "the most dramatic sea change in clinical medicine" that she had ever seen (Dominus).

The risks were overstated, according to Dr. Stephanie Faubion, director of the Mayo Clinic Center for Women's Health. She noted that women who were given a combination of estrogen and progestin didn't see an increase in risk for five years, and even after 20 years the mortality rate for women on HRT was no greater than the control group. Similarly, the risk of embolism was no greater than taking oral contraceptives or being pregnant.

But the real problem with the W.H.I study was that women in their 50s, who tend to be healthier but also have more menopausal symptoms, were underrepresented in the study. The average age of the subjects was 63. Women in their 50s have a lower risk of clots and stroke, so the risk from taking hormones is also lower. A closer analysis of the age of subjects showed that women under 60 had no elevated risk of heart disease with hormones. However, women over 60 did show an increased risk of heart disease, and women over 70 had an even greater risk. Researchers speculate that hormones used within a certain window of time, before declines in health associated with age occur, may preserve health, whereas hormones prescribed later may actually accelerate decline.

Despite this speculation, no research has been done on women who start hormones in their 50s and continue into their 60s, a research lacuna that gives no clear guidance for women in this age group, who are being overlooked despite the benefits that hormone therapy could provide. Their well-being is simply not considered important enough. In addition, "there hasn't been a single randomized trial of hormone therapy for women in perimenopause," says Pauline Maki, professor of psychiatry at the University of Illinois in Chicago. "Egregious, right?" she asks (Dominus).

Even with the research findings that are available, "menopause has the worst P.R. campaign in the history of the universe," says Dr. Rachel Rubin, assistant clinical professor at Georgetown University (Dominus). She suggests that more doctors proactively go over a list of menopausal symptoms with their middle-aged patients to inquire whether they are symptomatic, rather than waiting for their patients to initiate a discussion of a syndrome they may know little about.

To make matters worse, medical schools often overlook menopause in their curricula. Since many residents began training after the W.H.I. study, which led to the idea that HRT is dangerous, many of them received little to no education about menopause. A 2017 study showed that a third of residents said they would not prescribe hormones to symptomatic women even in the absence of risk factors (Dominus). Adequate treatment for such women is available but underutilized.

The situation is worse for Black women, who are more often overlooked in the treatment of menopause. They tend to start menopause earlier, have worse symptoms, and receive less treatment (Eldred, 2023). The effect of structural racism on disparities in menopause treatment has not been adequately taken into account or addressed. Black women receive prescriptions for hormone treatment from their doctors at half the rate of white women (Marsh et al., 1999).

It appears that Black women's symptoms are being minimized or dismissed to an even greater extent than those of white women. Further study needs to be done to establish what factors are creating racial inequities, including discrimination by doctors prescribing hormones.

Seventy to 80% of women experience hot flashes during menopause, some for as long as 14 years, as a result of diminishing levels of estrogen. Black women, unsurprisingly, have the most hot flashes (Gupta, A., 2023). A new drug to treat hot flashes, called Veozah, came onto the market in May 2023. However, unless doctors are more attuned to women's suffering and more willing to prescribe it, it will not make a significant difference.

In an online support group for women who received treatment remotely through a site called Alloy, women vented about "how hard it was for them to find relief, how much they still are suffering or how traumatized they still are by the lack of compassion and concern they encountered when seeking help for distressing symptoms" (Dominus, 2023). Feminists must demand that their menopause symptoms be taken seriously and continue to press for adequate treatment for a syndrome that jeopardizes their health and quality of life. Treatment already exists that can reduce or eliminate needless suffering, but only if doctors are willing to use it.

Gender Data Gap

One reason women, especially women of color, are not receiving adequate health care is because research studies do not include them. Men are considered the default, leaving women to be lumped in with them because researchers do not realize how different women's bodies really are. Women are not just smaller men. Research that doesn't include women is often presented as gender-neutral. Either data is not collected on women or data is not separated by sex. Data about women of color, disabled, and working-class women is simply not available.

The gender data gap in medical research is a major problem underlying the inadequate medical treatment of women. Because researchers didn't see differences between the sexes, aside from size and reproductive function, they conducted their research almost exclusively on men. The results were presented as applicable to both men and women, even when women were not included in the studies. Researchers have argued that including women in studies is a waste of resources and that women's bodies are too complicated, prone to skewing the data in unpredictable ways (note the assumption that women's bodies are too wily to be pinned down scientifically). Another argument against including women is that they are too hard to recruit, although when efforts are made, women enroll just as frequently as men (Sauro, 2024).

Even when women are included in studies, researchers often fail to sex-disaggregate the data, which makes no sense. Some progress has been made in eliminating data gaps. In 1993, the National Institutes of Health required that women be included in federally funded trials, but it has been difficult to know whether the NIH is enforcing that rule. Furthermore, the rule applies only to federally funded studies, which leaves the field wide open for independent research (N.I.H., 2024). The net result of the failure to include women is that they are experiencing side effects from medications that were not found in men, sometimes even fatalities. And gender-neutral doses of medication can cause overdoses in women. Treatments for diseases in women are not being adequately researched, with the result that some treatments may not help and may even harm.

Another egregious case of the gender data gap affecting medical care for women is the lack of research and funding for many disabling diseases that are more prevalent in women, such as rheumatoid arthritis, multiple sclerosis, and myalgic encephalomyelitis/chronic fatigue syndrome. Because these diseases affect women more than men, they have been undervalued in the world of medical research. The misogynistic assumptions embedded in "scientific" research need to be uncovered and ferreted out so that the patriarchal roots of the medical field are removed. Feminists, not content to suffer in silence from the damaging effects of being excluded from medical research, must raise their voices on this issue and demand equal inclusion in medical studies.

Design of Cars

Another issue relating to the gender data gap that has a profound impact on women's safety, but at the same time is less well-known by both women and men, is the design of cars. Crash tests, first introduced in the 1950s, have been performed primarily on male dummies, despite the fact that women are more likely than men to be seriously or moderately injured in crashes (71 and 47% respectively) and are 17% more likely to die (Shaver, 2012). Men are, on average, taller and heavier, with greater muscle mass and higher bone density, all of which affect how their bodies behave in crash tests.

For instance, women tend to sit closer to the steering wheel when driving because they are shorter and have more trouble reaching the pedals; they also sit up straighter to see over the dashboard. As a result, in frontal collisions they are more likely to sustain internal as well as leg injuries. And because women's neck and shoulder muscles are not as large as men's, they have three times the rate of whiplash in rear-end collisions. Seat design is also a factor in whiplash. Seats that have been tested on male dummies are firmer, and because they don't absorb the shock of impact, they tend to throw women forward.

I can offer personal testimony about the dangers of whiplash in rear-end collisions. When coming home on a highway after visiting relatives for Thanksgiving, I was a passenger in a car that was rear-ended. The crash caused me to be thrown forward suddenly. I was taken to the nearest emergency room by ambulance and diagnosed with whiplash. I was given neck exercises to do at home and discharged. Throughout the following week I suffered from headaches, nausea, and occasional lack of orientation to place. After a week of completing my usual work duties but not feeling back to normal, I decided I needed to see my primary care physician and request a CAT scan (which had not been performed in the ER). My doctor agreed to order the scan, and immediately upon seeing the results, she told me to go to the nearest hospital. There I was hooked up to IV anesthesia, and when I awoke, I found that my head had been shaved and tubes were draining blood from my brain. The whiplash had caused a subdural hematoma, and the CAT scan showed that my brain had been pushed into the right hemisphere by blood that had filled the left hemisphere. I feel sure that if I hadn't gone to my PCP when I did, I would have died.

The whole episode was traumatic, but I have recovered completely. My partner was driving the car at the time of the accident, and my dog was in the back seat. Both were unscathed. I am a short person and never felt I fit properly in the car we were driving. The headrest was too high, and the seat belt was choking me. The seat may not have been spongy enough to absorb the shock of the impact and may have thrown me forward. I now know firsthand what can happen to women passengers who are injured in crashes, most likely as a result of car design that does not take account of the differences of women's bodies. My anger about my injury, as well as the negligence of the ER which discharged me without proper testing, has motivated me to write about the issue of car design. It matters.

In 2011, some car manufacturers started to use female-sized dummies. *The Washington Post* reported that Beth Milito and her husband bought a 2011 Toyota Sienna primarily because of its five-star safety rating (Shaver, 2012). They discovered later that the passenger seat had only a two-star rating because of the change to female dummies. That meant that in a 35 mph frontal collision, a female passenger had a 20-40% chance of being killed or seriously injured, whereas vehicles in that class had on average a 15% risk. Milito stated that when her family is traveling in the car, she's the one in the passenger seat, which left her without the protection she sought from buying that vehicle.

In 2015, a report by the Insurance Institute for Highway Safety proudly reported that better vehicle design had brought down death rates. What the report failed to mention was that only drivers were studied, not passengers. Since women are typically passengers, the study essentially eliminated women—a serious gender gap in data collection.

Pregnant women are even more overlooked in the design of cars. Although pregnant dummies have been available since

1996, they are not commonly used and are not required for government tests. Seat belts don't fit well for them and can ride up, especially later in pregnancy, exposing fetuses to fatal trauma during car accidents. Seat belts also don't fit well for enlarged breasts during pregnancy and may increase the risk of injury when improperly worn.

Today male dummies are still the standard in driver seats and female dummies in passenger seats, leaving women without meaningful data to assess their risk as drivers. Congress had been attempting to persuade the Biden administration to address the gender gap in crash test safety data rather than push for electric cars. Supporters of the 2023 House bill are outraged that federal dollars are not provided to prevent the deaths of hundreds of women every year in car crashes. Former U.S. Representative Susan Molinari (R-NY), co-chair of VERITY Now, a group advocating for gender parity in car safety, stated, "This is 2023, and we still don't have a [biorealistic] crash test dummy for females in cars. That is absolutely outrageous and stunning to me, that we are still fighting for equal representation" (Molinari & Brooke, 2021). The bill points out that the National Highway Traffic Safety Administration has been researching the issue for 15 years and that the time for action is "long overdue."

Rep. Rosa DeLauro (D-Conn) called for more funding for crash test safety data which is "critical [to] fight the gender inequity in vehicle safety and crash victims" (Molinari & Brooke). *Fox News* host Tucker Carlson made a horrifying and outrageous response to her: "Call us woke, but that seems like transphobia. Did it never occur to Congresswoman DeLauro to put lipstick on the male dummies and have them identify as female?" *The New York Post* chimed in: "Dum (sic) idea: [Pete] Buttigieg wants to spend $20 million on female crash dummies" (Guo, 2023). In fact, the U.S. Transportation Department, headed by Buttigieg, asked for $5 million. But statements by the *Post* and Carlson make both of them look like dummies.

A female dummy called THOR-5F has been researched for 20 years and has passed muster with the NHTSA as an anatomically correct model of adult females. It is ready for implementation in crash tests if funding is released. But NHTSA's proposed rules used for consumer safety ratings do not include using the THOR-5F, to the disappointment of its supporters. Instead, rulemaking by the NHTSA includes other new dummies that mimic the average adult male body.

Sen. Deb Fisher (R-Neb.) says she doesn't understand why the new female dummies are not being employed in crash tests. "Why aren't they [NHTSA] moving ahead?" she asks. "I don't know. But we're going to keep pressuring them" (Guo). Feminists need to pressure lawmakers as well. If new dummies more representative of women's bodies are not utilized, hundreds more women will suffer needless injuries and death. It doesn't get more serious than that.

CHAPTER NINE

Violence and Rage

"... women's anger is a molten pond at the core of me,
my most fiercely guarded secret. … How to train that anger
with accuracy rather than deny it has been one
of the major tasks of my life."
—Audre Lorde

Violence Against Women

Violence against women is one of the most pressing problems facing women today. Violence against women is rooted in religious orthodoxy that calls for women to be subordinate to men, even at risk to their own health and bodily integrity. Here, too, we see the influence of Judaeo-Christian theology, which stripped the fierce goddesses of their power and set the stage for all women to be seen as subordinate.

The World Health Organization estimates that three out of 10 women globally have experienced physical or sexual violence, and 27% of women between ages 15 and 49 report that such violence has occurred in a relationship with an intimate partner. In fact, approximately 38% of all murders of women are committed by intimate partners (World Health Organization, 2024). Globally, a woman is killed by a family member (often a parent or sibling, in the case of honor killings) every 11 minutes.

Many countries do not criminalize marital rape, including India, Bangladesh, The Republic of Congo, Iran, China, Afghanistan, and North Korea (Outlook, 2022). And although marital rape is now outlawed in all U.S. states, 12 states have exceptions that treat marital rape differently from other rape cases. In several states, such as Nevada, Oklahoma, and Nevada, marital rape must involve force; in Ohio, for example, marital rape is regarded as an offense only if the couple is not living together. In Virginia, perpetrators can receive counseling instead of punishment, which can leave the partner in danger (World Population Review, 2024). The failure to criminalize marital rape is derived from the notion that women are still considered the legal property of men, without the right to their own bodily autonomy.

In the U.S., domestic violence prepandemic was at a high, with 50 women a month, or one in three female victims of murder, killed by their intimate partners, and one in four women subjected to physical or sexual violence by their partners. The National Coalition Against Domestic Violence reported that domestic violence hotlines received over 20,000 calls per day. The pandemic caused many women to flee relationships characterized by violence (Griffith).

The Violence Against Women Act (VAWA), signed into law by President Clinton in 1994, provided housing for women needing protection from domestic abuse, focused on prevention of violence, and included the first federal criminal law pertaining to violence against women. It has been reauthorized several times, most recently in 2022, with additional protections for immigrants, Native women, and LGBTQA+ people. As a result of key provisions in the VAWA made by the Obama administration, domestic violence decreased by 35%, and intimate partner homicides decreased by 46% (Obama White House Archives, 2013). Although these reductions are important, more work still needs to be done to stop violence against women.

The nomination of Clarence Thomas to the Supreme Court in 1991 by President George H.W. Bush brought the issue of sexual harassment of women to the fore. Black lawyer and educator Anita Hill testified that when she worked for Thomas at the Education Department and the Equal Employment Opportunity Commission, he had made remarks about pubic hair, breasts, and penis size. Thomas played the race card, declining to "provide the rope for my own lynching" and claiming that her accusations invoked the stereotype of Black men as sexual predators; as a Black woman, Hill's testimony undercut Thomas's attempt to play the race card. Thomas was eventually sworn in at a private ceremony at the White House with no other justices in attendance (Griffith). Polling indicated that women were enraged that Congress did not believe Anita Hill; Ellen Malcolm, founder of EMILY's List and its president until 2010, said, "Anita Hill's courage … unleashed years of pent-up rage" (Griffith).

The #MeToo movement brought new awareness to the issue of sexual harassment and assault. The term "Me Too" was a mantra coined in 2006 by Tarana Burke, a Black activist from New York City. It registered with women around the globe, who chimed in that they too had been violated by men. The momentum it created led to many famous men being accused, including Roger Ailes and Bill O'Reilly of *Fox News*, comedian Bill Cosby, USA Gymnastics physician Larry Nassar, and film producer Harvey Weinstein. All were fired from their jobs, resigned, or were convicted of criminal charges (although Cosby's conviction was overturned).

The high-profile 2022 case of an antidefamation suit brought by actor Johnny Depp against his actress wife, Amber

Heard, brought the issue of women's credibility in reporting sexual abuse to the forefront again. Depp claimed that Heard had defamed him in an op-ed she wrote for *The Washington Post* in 2018 about surviving domestic violence, which did not mention Depp by name. In her article, she expressed support for women experiencing domestic violence and stated, "We have an opening now to bolster and build institutions protective of women. For starters, Congress can reauthorize and strengthen the Violence Against Women Act" (Rosenblatt, 2022).

The jury did not believe Heard's account of domestic violence perpetrated against her by Depp, finding that she acted with malice and ruling for Depp. Afterward, Heard stated her disappointment with the verdict and what it means for women: "It is a setback. It sets back the clock to a time when a woman who spoke up and spoke out could be publicly shamed and humiliated" (Rosenblatt). More than 130 people wrote a letter of support for Heard, including Gloria Steinem and representatives of organizations such as NOW (the National Organization of Women), the National Women's Law Center, Equality Now, and the Women's March Foundation. The letter spoke of the rising misuse of defamation lawsuits to silence women who speak out about domestic violence and questioned why organizations that had supported victims during the #MeToo movement were now silent. Nevertheless, those who did speak out were subjected to a backlash by Depp's supporters.

During the trial Heard alleged that Depp raped her with a liquor bottle during a fight about his drinking and cut off the tip of his finger with the bottle as he broke it. As part of the backlash against her, a sex toy company, Twisted Fantasies, created a dildo that looked like a liquor bottle, a horrifying example of how a company with a profit motive capitalized on Heard's story of sexual abuse—and an example of how capitalism and patriarchy are intertwined (MaylayMail, 2022). In addition, a bakery called Dessert Boxes sent Heard a cake of a hand with a finger missing, along with a bottle of liquor. They posted a video of the package on TikTok with the caption "We're sending Amber Heard a box." The video was viewed 550,00 times and drew 15,000 likes as of May 2022 (Herbert, 2022). These twisted responses to Amber Heard's account of her sexual violation highlight the pressing work feminists still need to do to counter misogynist views that are so prevalent in society.

The Power of Reclaiming Rage

In our society women are conditioned to internalize their anger, which then manifests as depression and many health-related conditions. They are encouraged to tamp down their anger in the interest of being accommodating and pliable, virtues that are deemed suitable for their gender. However, anger that is suppressed or repressed tends to turn against one's body and mind, resulting in higher levels of depressed mood, somatization, autoimmune disorders, suicide, and diminished energy. Suppressed anger occurs when angry feelings are intentionally avoided or pushed down, whereas repressed anger happens when the process is unconscious. Women are twice as likely as men to experience depression, a finding documented in many cultures and countries around the world (Malhi & Mann, 2018).

When we swallow our rage and anger rather than expressing it in a healthy and efficacious manner, it has a toxic effect on the body. Numerous scientific studies point to suppressed/repressed anger as causes for diseases such as breast cancer, cardiovascular disease, and multiple sclerosis (Chapman, 2013). Anger and rage that are pushed down into our psyches can also result in pain syndromes in our body, without our being aware of their etiology (Davis, 2022). People in pain may then turn to opiates to help them tolerate the pain, often resulting in opiate abuse, addiction, and even death. Allowing anger and rage to surface in healthy ways, perhaps with the assistance of psychotherapy, can have an ameliorative effect on pain and other physical illnesses.

In my practice as a clinical psychologist, I have worked with many women who have fallen into depression because they are unable to access and express their anger. Mary, whose last name is omitted for the sake of confidentiality, began therapy with me in her early 20s as a college graduate. She had presented with chronic depression since middle school, with frequent episodes of crying, panic attacks, passive suicidal ideation, and acute feelings of worthlessness. Despite her education, Mary worked as a clerk in a grocery store. Her hobbies included knitting and writing poetry. She felt she was a burden to everyone in her life, taking up resources as a sad person and calling herself a "needy bitch."

Mary was in a "solid" relationship with a man she was living with. Her relationship with her mother was reported as good, but her father had frequently fat-shamed her and criticized many aspects of her lifestyle and appearance, including tattoos and brightly colored hair. She had been her father's favorite until the age of 13, when he emotionally withdrew from her upon her reaching puberty. At that time, she felt no one loved or appreciated her and blamed herself for that situation.

Mary was prescribed an antidepressant and experienced some improvement of her depression, including a slight elevation of her mood and decreased crying jags. She began to own the anger she felt toward her father and acknowledged her resentment at trying to be the type of person he wanted her to be, which included being academically outstanding and good at sports, neither of which she excelled at. Calling herself "stupid" and "embarrassing," she had clearly internalized her father's blame and disappointment in her.

Eventually, Mary began to express her anger about her father's treatment of her, especially his demeaning comments about her weight, eating habits, and perceived lack of exercise. She started to set boundaries with him about questions he asked regarding those issues. Looking back at her younger self, she acknowledged that she had been neglected and verbally abused by her father. She admitted that she could never get through to him and realized she deserved better than he could ever give her. She allowed herself to feel grief and anger about his treatment of her and discovered that it helped.

In a pivotal session, she let herself cry and felt the full weight of her anger at her father for not accepting her for who she is/was. She realized she had not done anything wrong and stated, "I deserve better. I deserve having my needs met." She wrote several other affirmations to use at home about being entitled to all her feelings, in their full breadth and depth. She now loves her 13-year-old self, even though she didn't feel loved at the time. She created a checklist of questions to use in discerning healthy from unhealthy relationships in her life, including: Are you giving more than you're receiving? Is the other person able to communicate? Are they able to accept me for who I am? Finally, she concluded: "I feel like I don't shove things down like I used to. Anger is giving me clarity."

Barbara is a 65-year-old single female living with her partner. She entered therapy after the death of her mother from dementia. She presented with generalized anxiety disorder with hypervigilance, an autoimmune disorder (Hashimoto's disease), panic attacks, painful constipation, and overeating when stressed. Barbara was grieving the loss of her mother but also feeling free to be herself for the first time in her life. Her mother, whom she describes as narcissistic, frequently belittled her, asking, "Who do you think you are?" whenever Barbara expressed her own thoughts or feelings. Her mother had an overeating disorder, consuming any leftover food in the household during the night. Barbara never felt nurtured by her and was in fact expected to be her mother's caretaker. She recounted times when her mother would scream at her and destroy her stuffed animals if she woke up during the night.

Barbara had repressed her anger at her mother, fearing that if she expressed it, her mother would yell or criticize her. Therapy focused on helping her tap into and express anger at her mother in a healthy manner, which she gradually became more comfortable with. She wrote a mock letter venting her anger at her mother and in several sessions expressed anger that no one in her family came to her rescue when her mother was abusive.

Eventually, her symptoms improved; her anxiety and hypervigilance decreased, her constipation improved, her panic attacks diminished, and her stress eating declined. Since the psychological literature shows a connection between repressed anger and autoimmune conditions, Barbara's treatment will continue to focus on helping her connect to the anger which has lived in the shadow of her psyche, with the hope that doing so will contribute to the improvement of her health and well-being, especially her Hashimoto's.

Sandra is a 34-year-old married woman who presented with generalized and social anxiety as well as moderate depression. She reported trouble getting out of bed in the morning, lying on the couch on weekends, and lack of motivation to exercise. Sandra's mother died when she was 10, leaving her to take care of two younger siblings, as well as her father, who was not coping well with his grief. She submerged her grief about her mother's death in order to take on the role of caretaker and mediator in the family. Sandra's therapy focused on helping her grieve the loss of her mother; anger, the second stage of grief, surfaced in the process. She had been completely unaware of her anger, as she was so involved in taking care of other people's needs.

During the course of treatment, Sandra decided it was time to start a family. She told her gynecologist that she had suffered from heavy cramps and bleeding for several years. Her doctor ordered an ultrasound, which revealed fibroids. Sandra responded to this news with her recently discovered anger. She had complained for years to her doctors about her symptoms. None of the doctors bothered to order tests to see what was wrong, perhaps because doctors tend not to take women's pain seriously, assuming it must be in their heads. Meanwhile, Sandra had been trying unsuccessfully to get pregnant for about a year. She realized that the fibroids had probably prevented her from getting pregnant. She decided to have surgery to remove the fibroids. The surgery was successful, and Sandra became pregnant afterward. However, she still felt angry that no doctor had taken her seriously enough to order tests.

Sandra's depression has lifted as a result of getting in touch with her anger. She now brings energy and motivation to everyday tasks. She reports feeling that the dark cloud which had hung over her head has lifted. Her self-care has improved, and she has removed herself from the mediating/caretaking role with her family. The grief work in therapy moved her toward a greater acceptance of her mother's death. The process of uncovering her own feelings, especially her anger, has brought Sandra a newfound sense of equilibrium and well-being.

Anger is often portrayed as a negative emotion that is destructive to those who experience it as well as those who are on the receiving end. And while that might be true for some cases of anger and rage expressed in extreme or out-of-control outbursts by so-called "rageaholics," anger and rage are normal responses to perceived wrongs in our environment. All of us are programmed to experience anger as part of a repertoire of healthy responses to boundary violations and unjust or unfair situations. It is an appropriate reaction that lets people know they need to take action to remedy such wrongs. Anger motivates people to stand up for themselves and speak out against violations of their rights. It becomes the fuel for movements to change society in ways that promote justice and fairness. Trusting our anger to reveal to us what most needs to change can be a valuable lesson. Those who deny their anger, believing that they need to respond only with love and compassion in all situations, are engaging in spiritual bypass.

Spiritual Bypass

The term "spiritual bypass" was coined in the 1980s by John Welwood, a psychotherapist and Buddhist teacher. It refers to using spirituality to avoid facing uncomfortable issues on a personal, interpersonal, or systemic level. Suppressing negative emotions in favor of "looking on the bright side" closes off a whole range of experience which can be necessary for growth. Sometimes, indeed often, life is painful and difficult, and trying to sidestep such pain and discomfort with the notion that everything happens for a reason prevents coming to terms with the reality of the situation. The belief that life is unfolding perfectly is a form of denial; it denies the very real suffering in the world and all the things that need to be changed. Those who purport to be so spiritually enlightened that they cannot see the injustices that need to be addressed through activism have an illusory worldview. The idea that everything is operating as it should according to a spiritual world order is a chimera. Those who engage in spiritual bypass are looking at life through rose-colored glasses that distort the full measure of experience, including negative emotions. They judge those who become angry about injustice as spiritual inferiors who dwell on negativity. But looking down on the cruelties and barbarities of life in such a detached way, eliminating them from the scope of true reality, becomes a form of toxic positivity.

But isn't positivity a good thing, a way of helping us "rise above" the bad or unfortunate things that happen to us? Doesn't it buffer our negative experiences in ways that enable us to survive life's vicissitudes? A certain amount of positivity can be useful in creating hope that things can be better, and people do need hope to avoid falling into cynicism and despair. But positivity becomes toxic when it avoids looking at very real problems that need to be addressed. And without the awareness of what is wrong, no change can happen. Toxic positivity stifles efforts to engage in change-making behaviors when it denies that pain, suffering, and injustice exist. Negative emotions such as grief and anger, whether in our personal lives or in relation to our social structure, are a sign that work needs to be done.

Spiritual bypass can be buttressed by spiritual or religious beliefs such as "God is taking care of everything" or "everything in the universe is proceeding as it should," but spiritual bypass does not depend on overt religious beliefs. It can simply take the form of being "nice" rather than calling out and confronting what is wrong and needs fixing. Women in our society have been acculturated to be nice and accommodating rather than confrontive and assertive. Being nice can lead to complacency, to accepting things as they are rather than fighting for something better. Women too often fall into the complacency trap when they try to meet society's expectations of being "nice"—passive, conforming, and pleasant. Indoctrinating women with such cultural expectations robs them of their own agency in making changes in their own lives and in society. When women avoid or suppress their anger, they are deprived of the motivating power of their own rage. They are cut off from the shadow side of their psyches, which is just as valid and life-enhancing as the "enlightened" part of the psyche that lives in the conscious mind.

Women who have defied society's expectations by proactively seeking equal rights in the feminist movement have been disparaged as "feminazis," a term used pejoratively by conservative radio talk show host Rush Limbaugh to describe women who, he says, have a "quest for power" and a "belief that men aren't necessary." Limbaugh portrayed women on the front lines battling for their rights as man-haters who "are obsessed with perpetuating a modern-day holocaust: abortion" (Young, 2021). Women who dare to fight for bodily autonomy and equality with men are thus vilified as harpies engaging in a power grab from men. It is not surprising, then, that women would want to shrink away from such vilification and retreat into safer cultural spaces such as homemaking and caretaking, in which they are perceived as less militant.

The retreat of women into the safety of culturally conforming attitudes and behaviors has been a factor limiting their exploration of their shadow side, depriving them of owning their righteous indignation at a system that perpetuates their oppression. In this sense, cultural constraints on women's power have operated as a form of "spiritual" bypass for them, in which women accept their prescribed roles in society and suppress or repress their anger at being disempowered.

In American society, women's culturally prescribed behavior is often sanctioned by religion, making it overtly a form of spiritual bypass. Christian ideologies encourage women to deny their subordinate status, as well as any related anger, and keep those who subscribe to them from demanding equality; for instance, it says in Ephesians: "Wives, submit yourselves to your own husbands as you do to the Lord. For the husband is the head of the wife as Christ is the head of the church, his body, of which he is the Savior. Now as the church submits to Christ, so also wives should submit to their husbands in everything" (Bible Gateway, New International Version). According to Genesis, woman was created as a helpmate to man. She was thus made subordinate to him, while he occupied the God-given role as head of the household.

For generations women have followed such biblical teachings, but doing so has often required them to negate their sense of self, giving rise to frustration and anger—sometimes consciously and sometimes not. Religiously prescribed roles, especially when adopted by women themselves, have served as forms of spiritual bypass, in which women deny or repress negative emotions associated with being subordinate.

In her book *The Feminine Mystique*, Betty Friedan describes "the problem that has no name"—the plight of housewives in the 1950s and '60s who lacked a sense of identity and purpose while trying to fulfill their roles as housewives and mothers. Friedan's book hit home with women of the time who were trapped in their domestic roles but often unaware of the suffering it caused them. In many cases they turned to tranquilizers to soothe their pain while enabling them to stay in their prescribed roles. The 1966 song "Mother's Little Helper" released by the Rolling Stones dovetailed with Friedan's writing about the plight of housewives who tried to fulfill their roles in the home, often at the expense of their mental health.

Friedan's book was an eye-opener for women and led to the second wave of feminism. Friedan became one of the founders of NOW (National Organization of Women), whose founding statement called for the full equality of all women and was "dedicated to the proposition that women first and foremost are human beings, who … must have the chance to develop their fullest human potential" (Friedan, 1963).

Despite Friedan's call for equality for all women, her book nevertheless addressed the concerns of white middle-class women without speaking to the needs of BIPOC, trans, or poor, working-class women. bell hooks remarked:

> Friedan did not tell readers whether it was more fulfilling to be a maid, a babysitter, a factory worker, a clerk, or a prostitute than to be a leisure-class housewife. She made her plight and the plight of white women like herself synonymous with a condition affecting all American women. In so doing, she deflected attention away from her classism, her racism, her sexist attitudes towards the masses of American women. In the context of her book, Friedan makes clear that the women she saw as victimized by sexism were college-educated white women" (hooks).

Despite her lack of intersectional analysis, Friedan set in motion a wave of feminism that helped many, if not all, women look at the shadow side of their psyches, at their anger and frustration, to explore what was missing in their lives and what needed to change on a structural level to ensure their full participation in society.

Anger can help women look beyond their own frustrations about their place in society to imagine a world in which structural transformations that enable their full participation can occur. Soraya Chemaly aptly points out that anger is "one of the most hopeful and forward thinking of all our emotions. It begets transformation, manifesting our passion and keeping us invested in the world" (Chemaly, 2018).

Black activist and author Audre Lorde says, "Anger is loaded with information and energy" (Lorde, 2007). She confides that her response to racism is anger and affirms its value in challenging oppressive systems: "Focused with precision [anger] can become a powerful source of energy serving progress and change. And when I speak of change, I do not mean a simple switch of positions or a temporary lessening of tensions, nor the ability to smile or feel good. I am speaking of a basic and radical alteration in those assumptions underlining our lives" (Lorde). Lorde is clearly calling for a form of radical feminism that changes our basic social structure and patriarchal assumptions.

On a similar note, June Jordan, Black poet and activist, proclaimed, in "Rage for Our Daughters," "I do not believe that we can restore and expand the freedoms that our lives require unless and until we embrace the justice of our rage … through the expression of an emotion that for millennia has been deemed unacceptable for women. An emotion that even today causes women to be labeled 'bat-shit crazy.' A wise emotion, here to tell us that SOMETHING IS WRONG."

She asks, "How do we exercise the fundamental human right of autonomy over our bodies? [Her answer:] Rage."

"How do we rid ourselves of shame? Rage."

"How do we move through the world with the confidence to express ourselves and our position? Rage."

She calls for women not to surrender their rights "without a face full of fury" (Jordan, 2003).

Medusa

Art and image © Lydia Ruyle.

CHAPTER TEN

Nasty Women

"I'm a nasty woman—a loud, vulgar, proud woman."
—words by Nina Donovan, 19-year-old from Tennessee,
read by Ashley Judd at the 2017 Women's March
after the inauguration of Donald Trump

Medusa

The Greek myth of Medusa has captured the female imagination of a figure who embodies the rage of women who have been violated and demonized. As the daughter of chthonic sea gods Keto and Phorkys, Herodotus placed her origin in Libya, which would make her dark-skinned. Medusa had two Gorgon sisters, Stheno and Euryale, but she was the only mortal of the three. Even though Medusa is not considered a goddess, she was a powerful female figure from Greek mythology who looked a great deal like Kali and had many of the same powers. She is depicted with a fearsome face, staring eyes, protruding tongue, and exposed teeth, often fangs. In spite of these similarities, scholars have not linked them, as they seem to have emerged separately in different cultures. But even without one culture inspiring another, different cultures came up with similar archetypes, which strengthens the idea that the fierce goddesses are present in all of us.

Scholar Jane Harrison suggests that Medusa was actually the Goddess hiding behind a hideous apotropaic mask, intended to protect her sacred aspects from those who would profane them (Harrison, 1991). In Greek society, images of the head of Medusa were placed on graves, walls, coins, shields, and breastplates as powerful, protective symbols to ward off evil. And even though Medusa is imbued with destructive powers by Athena, her image is preserved as a sort of amulet which protects against harm and the desacralization of society.

Like dark goddesses, Medusa has not only destructive but also life-giving powers. Blood from the left side of her body was instantly lethal, but blood from the right side of her body was healing. When Perseus cut off Medusa's head, the giant named Chrysaor, wielding a golden sword, and the beautiful, winged

Etruscan, from Italy, 6th century B.C.E.
National Museum of Scotland, Edinburgh

https://en.wikipedia.org/wiki/Medusa#/media/File:Roof_ornament_with_Medusa's_head._Etruscan,_from_Italy,_6th_century_BCE._National_Museum_of_Scotland,_Edinburgh.jpg. CC BY-SA 4.0 International (https://creativecommons.org/licenses/by-sa/4.0/)

horse, Pegasus, sprang from the blood of her neck, illustrating the regenerative effects of her blood. Athena gave some of Medusa's blood to Asclepius, the god of medicine and healing, because of its healing properties.

According to Greek myth, Medusa was a beautiful maiden who was raped by Poseidon in Athena's temple. Athena, a patriarchal and warlike goddess who was born from her father Zeus's head, decided to punish Medusa by turning her into an ugly, hideous figure with snakes for hair who would turn any man who looked at her into stone. This myth sounds familiar today, when women who are raped are often vilified and blamed for their own violation.

However, Medusa's visage never turned women into stone, only men. Her frightening face can be construed as a response to the "male gaze," which objectifies and sexualizes women. If any man did that to Medusa, he would be met with a gaze that was potent and lethal. Images of Medusa typically show her gazing directly at the viewer, unlike most images of Greek faces, which are depicted at an angle.

The term "male gaze" was coined by film theorist Laura Mulvey in 1973 to explain how women were often depicted in films, specifically as passive objects who appealed to men's sexual fantasies and desires. Of course, the term did not exist at the time the myth of Medusa originated, but the male gaze was undoubtedly part of patriarchal society, which diminished the power of women and led to their being seen as sexual objects. The story of Medusa illustrates the power of the male gaze, as Poseidon looked upon her as a sexual object and raped her. And although Athena turned her into a monster, and victimized her again, Athena's "medicine" for Medusa had the effect of repelling men with a female gaze—perhaps a protective gesture for Medusa, who no longer had to fear being victimized by men.

Perseus was charged by King Polydectes with killing Medusa; the King hoped to send Perseus out of the way while he pursued Perseus's mother, Danae. And the King thought, of course, that Perseus would die from the encounter when he looked at Medusa. But, supplied with a scythe from Hermes and a mirrored shield from Athena, Perseus slayed Medusa by looking at her reflection in the shield rather than gazing at her directly. The slaying of Medusa is thought by some scholars to be a mythical representation of the invasion of Greece around 2000 B.C.E. by the patriarchal Hellenes, who wiped out the prevalent worship of the Goddess in her generic form.

Although Medusa ultimately dies, vanquished by a patriarchal figure, she becomes a symbol of fierce feminine energy that is potent enough to bring about the destruction of men who would violate women. The feminist writer Emily Erwin Culpepper wrote in an article titled "Gorgons: A Face for Contemporary Women's Rage," published in the fall 1986 issue of the magazine *Women of Power*: "The Amazon Gorgon face is female fury personified. The Gorgon/Medusa image has been rapidly adopted by large numbers of feminists who recognize her as one face of our own rage" (Culpepper, 1986).

Despite her hideous appearance, Medusa has become a heroine of sorts for many women who are outraged by their subordinate status and victimization in patriarchy. In the feminist journal *Women: A Journal of Liberation*, the editors identified Medusa as "a map to guide us through our terrors, through the depths of our anger into the sources of our power as women" (Rupp et al., 1978). Medusa has survived through the centuries because she continues to speak to women. Steven Wilk, author of *Medusa: Solving the Mystery of the Gorgon,* believes that Medusa's longevity owes to her serving as a fearsome protector of women: "Only the Gorgon has the savage, threatening appearance to serve as an immediately recognized symbol of rage and a protector of women's secrets" (Wilk, 2007).

Medusa made an appearance during the 2016 election as a vilified Hillary Clinton. Trump cast her as a Medusa monster who needed to be defeated. A Triumph T-shirt showed Trump, sword in hand, holding the severed head of Clinton, modeled on the statue of Perseus holding the head of Medusa by Benvenuto Cellini. The misogyny at play in the election was apparent in Trump's calls to "lock her up" and in the rape culture personified by Trump in his strident admission of "pussy grabbing," as well as several outstanding accusations of rape against him. Trump, full of vitriol, demonized Clinton as "the devil" and called her "a nasty woman." Elizabeth Johnston, in her article in *The Atlantic* in 2016, quipped that Medusa was "the original nasty woman" (Johnston, 2016). The myth of Medusa is still alive and well, with many women today taking on the mantle of "nasty woman" as a protest against the misogynistic labeling of Clinton during the election.

Medusa still makes her appearance in modern times. The fashion designer Versace made the face of Medusa the logo of his brand because he remembered it from the ruins he played in as a child in southern Italy. Now the Medusa face appears on each handbag in the Versace line, the same face that was engraved on the door of Versace's first headquarters in Milan. The logo appears on Versace products for men as well as women, a reminder of Medusa's universal appeal as a cultural icon over the centuries. Medusa also lives today on the flag of Sicily, which shows a figure with three legs in rotational symmetry, called a trinacria, with the head of winged Medusa in the middle surrounded by three ears of wheat. The figure appeared on coins from Syracuse in the fourth century B.C.E., when Sicily was ruled by Greece. Once again, Medusa endures as a protective figure, in this case protecting the island of Sicily, showing that a woman can be powerful enough to protect an entire country across the ages.

The Harpies

Also from Greek mythology, the Harpies are powerful female figures who are instruments of divine justice. Even though they are not goddesses, they resemble many of the dark goddesses in their fierce demeanor and destructive power. Known as "the hounds of Zeus," they are sent by him to snatch wrongdoers from the earth. Any sudden disappearances are attributed to the Harpies.

As the personification of strong storm winds, the Harpies are composed of three or four women: Aello, known as Storm Swift; Ocypete, Swift Wing; Podrage, Fleet Foot; and Celaeno, Dark Cloud. They are the daughters of the sea god Thaumas and the cloud nymph Electra, who, as the daughter of the Trojan war hero Agamemnon, is human. Early versions of the myths of the Harpies depict them as beautiful women with the wings and talons of birds of prey. Later versions show them as women with hideously ugly faces and the lower bodies of raptors, or entirely as birds of prey.

The transition from beauties to monsters may reflect the evolution of Greece from matriarchy to patriarchy during the Bronze Age from 3200 to 1200 B.C.E. In the eighth century B.C.E., Hesiod described the Harpies in his poem "Theogony" as "lovely haired creatures." By the third century B.C.E., however, Apollonius Rhodius referred to them as monsters with beaks in his epic poem "Argonautica."

The most well-known story about the Harpies concerns Phineas, King of Thrace, whom Zeus blinded and sent to an uninhabited island as punishment for revealing the secrets of the gods. Zeus provided a large buffet for Phineas every night but sent the Harpies, who had insatiable hunger, to snatch Phineas's food away from him before he could eat it. They befouled any scraps that remained and left a horrible smell in their wake.

Jason and the Argonauts were on their quest for the Golden Fleece when they came upon the starving Phineas. Among them were the Boreads, winged sons of the north wind. Phineas offered to share divine insights that would help them find their way in exchange for their getting rid of the Harpies. The Boreads Zetes and Calais attacked the Harpies and were about to kill them when the Harpies' sister Iris, personification of the rainbow, intervened and asked that their lives be spared. The Harpies agreed to leave Phineas alone if they were set free and returned to their home on the islands of Strophades.

As this story illustrates, the Harpies were instruments of divine retribution, a reminder that defying the gods has consequences. The Harpies are terrifying figures, but like the fierce goddesses, they act destructively when it is necessary to deliver divine justice.

The Furies

Like the Harpies, these goddesses from Greek mythology are fearsome creatures who live in the Underworld but travel to the earth to carry out divine retribution against sinners. Their parents are Gaia and Uranus, gods of earth and heaven. They were born from the blood shed when Gaia, angry at Uranus for imprisoning their children, convinced his son Cronus to castrate him; their names were Allecto (meaning anger), Megaera (jealousy), and Tisiphone (avenger).

The winged Furies were ugly creatures who wore black, tattered clothing and, like Medusa, had snakes for hair; their symbol was blood. They reported to Persephone, who used them to mete out justice from the Underworld. First written about in Homer's *Iliad* in the eighth century B.C.E., they were compared to personified curses or ghosts of murdered people.

The punishments the Furies carried out, although cruel, were fair, directed against those who disobeyed the gods or broke oaths. They were especially motivated to punish murderers of parents and older siblings, as they themselves were the product of family violence. The Furies used whips to inflict punishment but also drove people to madness, often by singing songs that tortured them with their own guilt. Despite being monsters, the Furies were worshipped, and people made sacrifices to them in a grove outside Athens that was dedicated to them.

As described in *Oresteia* by Aeschylus, the Furies pursued Orestes for the murder of his mother, Clytemnestra. He sought revenge on her for the murder of his father, Agamemnon, whom Clytemnestra killed for sacrificing their daughter Iphigenia to the gods during the Trojan War to ensure favorable winds for sailing. She also wished to take over the throne from Agamemnon with her lover Aegisthus. Spurred on by his sister Electra, and commanded by Apollo, Orestes murdered his mother and Aegisthus.

The Furies pursued him, but Apollo made them fall asleep while Orestes fled to Athens to seek help from Athena. She decided to call off the Furies in favor of a trial for him with a jury of citizens. In doing so, she established a legal form of redress for wrongs in Greece, which took the place of punishment by the vigilante goddesses of divine justice. The Furies acted as prosecutor, and Apollo served as defense. The jury was split, and Athena cast the tie vote for Orestes, who was acquitted and then fled to Delphi to be purified of his crime. Athena convinced the Furies to accept the verdict and disbanded them, renaming them the Eumenides, or "gracious ones," as they were no longer violent.

The renaming of the Furies from monsters to Eumenides reflects the transition to a patriarchal society as dictated by Athena, a patriarchal goddess born from her father Zeus's head. And it highlights the fact that under patriarchy women must become "gracious" and meek like the transformed Furies or risk being scorned and killed like Medusa.

CHAPTER ELEVEN

Integrating the Shadow

"The unconscious wants truth. It ceases to speak to those who want something else more than truth."
—Adrienne Rich

For women to escape the fate of being demonized as whores or sanitized as virgins, we need to explore and own our shadow sides. Only when our shadows are integrated can we become whole people living authentically, rejecting roles foisted on us by society. Baba Yaga, a fierce Slavic crone goddess, provides a strong model for how to individuate and come into our own power. Although she is a fearsome goddess, she also displays a benevolent side which helps us integrate our dark sides to achieve wholeness.

Baba Yaga

As a grandmother ("baba" in Serbian, Croatian, Bosnian, and Bulgarian, or "babushka" in Russian or Polish), Baba Yaga possesses wisdom that she can impart, but anyone who wishes to receive it must have the courage to face her fearsome nature. It is unclear what "yaga" stands for; it may be related to the Serbian and Croatian "jeza," which means horror, shudder, or chill, or

Baba Yaga

Art and image © Lydia Ruyle.

Polish "jedza," meaning witch or evil woman. Baba Yaga is not an ancient goddess, as the first mention of her is in Mikhail Lomonosov's *Russian Grammar* in 1755. She also appeared on wood-block prints in the late 17th and early 18th century in Russia.

Baba Yaga is an enigmatic goddess who sometimes helps people and sometimes eats them. Her role with heroes is marked by ambiguity. Sometimes she is a villain, trying to harm them, whereas at other times she is a donor, giving aid and a magic tool or gift. Sometimes she is a hostile donor, seeking to kill the hero but failing and ultimately yielding the magic agent. Even when she takes the role of a donor, she approaches the hero in an ambiguous manner, threatening to eat them but changing course when rebuked or asked for hospitality (Johns, 2024).

Baba Yaga lives alone deep in the woods and is portrayed as ugly and wrinkled, with a prosthetic leg made of bone, a long nose and chin, and sharp iron teeth. Her living hut, which constantly turns (perhaps mimicking the turning of the Wheel of the Year, which she has power over), is propped up on chicken legs and surrounded by a fence of human bones topped by glowing skulls. Anyone who wishes to gain entrance to her hut must say the magic words to make it stop turning: "Hut, hut, turn your eyes to the forest, your gate to me, so I can go in and out." In the various stories about Baba Yaga, the protagonist, or hero, mysteriously knows the incantation without being prompted. Once inside, the hero encounters Baba Yaga's comments about the hero's Russian smell, which she finds disgusting since she is not a human.

Baba Yaga's oven cooks people, often children who wander into her domain; it is a portal that opens to the otherworld. As a liminal goddess steeped in magic, she lives on the boundary between life and death. Stretched out in her hut, she reaches from wall to wall, packed as tightly as a corpse in a coffin. She flies in a mortar, steered by a pestle, and covers her "tracks" with a broom. She also uses the mortar and pestle to grind up the bones of her victims.

Although Baba Yaga is a woman, she is sometimes described as a phallic mother, possessing masculine as well as feminine characteristics. The pestle, which resembles a phallus, is sometimes used as a weapon, but it fits into a mortar, a container that evokes female anatomy. Her nose, so long that it punctures the ceiling when she lies in her hut, is unmistakably a phallic symbol. Her bony prosthetic leg also has phallic connotations. The combination of male and female characteristics renders her a supremely powerful goddess, unlimited by gender norms.

Baba Yaga has three horsemen who serve her interests—Bright Day, Red Sun, and Black Night, each representing a time of day. Although they are warriors, each of whom operates during a part of the day, their power derives from Baba Yaga. They symbolize Baba Yaga's control over diurnal time, just as her turning hut symbolizes control over time as the earth turns around the sun. The horsemen are dressed in their respective colors—white, red, and black—and ride steeds in matching colors. Baba Yaga chooses new horsemen every 100 years and gives each of them a magical weapon that dissolves if the horseman is killed. Unlike Baba Yaga, who acts capriciously, the horsemen are governed by cosmological forces.

The horsemen make an appearance in one of the best-known fairy tales about Baba Yaga: "Vasilisa the Beautiful." Vasilisa was the only daughter of a merchant and his wife. When she was eight years old, Vasilisa's mother, knowing that she was dying, gave a rag doll to Vasilisa with instructions to give it food and drink whenever she needed help. She was to tell no one about the doll, not even her father. After her mother died, Vasilisa gave it a little to eat and drink, and it eased her grief. Soon her father remarried a woman with two daughters, hoping that she would make a good mother to Vasilisa. However, the woman was cruel to her and made her do all the household chores. With the help of her doll, Vasilisa was able to keep up with all her duties.

When Vasilisa came of age, suitors pursued her, but her stepmother turned them away, saying it was not appropriate for her to marry when her daughters had no suitors, as they were undesirable. One day, Vasilisa's father had to leave on a business trip. On that same day, his wife sold the house and moved to the edge of the forest where Baba Yaga lived. The stepmother planned to get rid of Vasilisa by sending her into the forest, hoping that she would come across Baba Yaga and be eaten by her. However, her plan failed, as Vasilisa fed the doll, which kept her safe. Finally, the stepmother concocted an excuse to send Vasilisa directly to Baba Yaga's hut. She put out all the lights in the house and told Vasilisa that she needed to fetch light from Baba Yaga. Vasilisa consulted the doll, which advised her to go.

As she walked toward Baba Yaga's hut, she passed each of the three horsemen as they were patrolling the area during their time of the day, but they didn't stop her. When she reached the hut, she asked Baba Yaga for light, but Baba Yaga said Vasilisa would have to complete a number of grueling tasks or be killed, including cooking and cleaning for her, as well as separating rotten grains of corn from intact ones.

Baba Yaga left for the day, and Vasilisa again encountered the three horsemen during their respective parts of the day, reminding her of the passage of time as well as Baba Yaga's power over her. As Vasilisa was feeling exhausted and hopeless about finishing her tasks, her doll told her to sleep and performed her chores for her. When Baba Yaga returned, she asked how Vasilisa was able to finish her jobs. When Vasilisa told her it was because of her "mother's blessing," Baba Yaga, who wanted nothing to do with blessings, threw her out of the hut with a lantern made from a skull containing burning coals to provide light to her stepfamily.

When Vasilisa returned to them, she discovered that, strangely, none of the lights her family had brought into the house had lasted, and the lantern she brought back burned the whole family to ashes. Baba Yaga had used her magic to help the girl, despite her initial threats. The story has a happy ending: Vasilisa moved to Moscow and worked for a cloth maker, becoming so skilled that the Tsar noticed her and later married her. The story suggests that Vasilisa is transformed by her foray into Baba Yaga's world of darkness and aggression, where she learns to own her rage about her treatment by her stepmother and stepsisters. No longer a compliant child who attempts to complete all the work assigned by her stepmother, she returns home with a magically destructive light which burns the family to death.

In this tale, Baba Yaga is a hostile donor; her approach is ambiguous, as she threatens to kill Vasilisa but reneges on her threat and provides help by giving her the wished-for object, the magical lantern. European folktale figures usually relate to heroes in a nonambiguous fashion—as straightforward donors, giving whatever item is requested. In this folktale, however, Baba Yaga behaves ambiguously, threatening harm but changing course when Vasilisa complies with Baba Yaga's demand that she complete challenging tasks.

Andreas Johns, a scholar of Slavic languages and literature, discusses the structural differences of fairy tales that Baba Yaga appears in: the donor type; the ambiguous (or hostile donor) type; and the villain type, causing harm. He notes that Baba Yaga often functions as a donor or hostile donor to young girls, whereas she almost never serves as a donor to young boys, acting mostly as a villain. By contrast, she often acts as a donor type to adult heroes.

Baba Yaga's role with adult heroines remains mostly ambiguous; there is only one tale in which she is simply a donor.

Baba Yaga's relationship to females, whether children or adults, remains roughly the same, characterized mostly by ambiguity. But her relationship to males changes dramatically, from villain with boys to donor with adult men. This change may relate to developmental changes in males, who have an easier time separating from mother figures. As they mature, they are less inclined to identify with their mothers because their sex is different. Undifferentiated as children, they may view Baba Yaga with fear, especially because, drawing from Freud, she has the power to castrate them; with this power over them, she manifests as an ogress. But as mature men, they meet her more on their own terms and engender respect from her, leading to her willingness to serve as a donor. "The omnipotent mother of infancy and early childhood is put in her place," says Johns. "The hero's (and less frequently, heroine's) assertive or aggressive stance…is also a way of maintaining the boundary between the self and the mother, a declaration that one has ended the infantile relationship to her" (Johns).

The function of stories relating to girls on their trajectory toward adulthood is different from boys, who have an easier time separating from their mothers en route to becoming full, individuated, selves. In order to accomplish the same task for girls, Baba Yaga needs to confront them with ambiguity. Her hostility requires girls to meet a challenge in order to receive a magical gift. Girls are thus initiated into adult femininity by overcoming the challenges Baba Yaga sets for them. Such initiation rituals become celebrations of a shared female identity. The Vasilisa fairy tale illustrates such an initiation. As a result of overcoming the challenge set by Baba Yaga, Vasilisa changes from a hapless young girl oppressed by her stepmother and stepsisters to an adult woman who leaves home, develops a career, and finds a mate, and a famous one at that.

As a maternal figure who demonstrates ambiguity with females, Baba Yaga manifests psychological ambivalence toward them—a combination of both positive and negative feelings. She shows hostility in her threats and demands of the female heroine but also positive affect in ultimately rendering the wished-for object. Psychologists consider maternal ambivalence to be a normal phenomenon that occurs because of conflicts between the needs of a child and the needs of a mother. Resentments may arise on the part of mothers when the demands of mothering seem too great.

No mother can be consistently loving and attentive; sometimes anger surfaces, and the mother inevitably experiences negative feelings toward her child. Research has shown that mothers have greater ambivalence toward their daughters, whereas fathers have greater ambivalence toward their sons (Pillemer et al., 2012). Mothers' greater ambivalence toward their daughters may help to explain Baba Yaga's mixed emotions and contradictory actions toward females that are not duplicated in her interactions with males.

The emphasis on the oral aggression of Baba Yaga, who is described as a cannibalistic ogress, may reflect the oral needs and aggression of frustrated infants, who may have fantasies of eating or biting their mothers. My interpretation of the Baba Yaga stories is that the oral aggression of people whose oral needs are unresolved, resulting in oral fixation, is projected onto the mother figure, who in turn wants to eat her children. The latent desire of orally fixated individuals to orally incorporate their mothers is unacceptable to them, so they project it onto their mothers and develop a fear of being orally incorporated by them. The Baba Yaga fairy tales help them work through their own fears of oral incorporation by their mothers. In the tales, protagonists often succeed in preventing Baba Yaga from eating them by acceding to her demands for performing arduous work or simply by requesting that she cook them a meal instead.

Baba Yaga herself seems to have an orally fixated personality. In one story, she sucks blood from a maiden's breasts, suggesting that she herself may easily fall into the role of a frustrated infant desiring the mother's breasts as a form of oral incorporation, although her vampiric tendencies in sucking blood are a perverted form of such incorporation. Baba Yaga can easily switch from frustrated and hungry infant to frustrated and hungry witch, revealing the underlying dynamics of her role as an ogress who eats children.

The fairy tales in which Baba Yaga appears have themes that concern mothering and its effects on the maturation or psychological development of children. The challenges and pitfalls of this process are highlighted and symbolically portrayed in these tales, which may operate on an unconscious level to help children master them. Even adult protagonists can relate to these stories, in which Baba Yaga as a grandmother figure can still have a significant influence on how their lives change and evolve. Our culture is hard on mothers, blaming them for any problems a child has, under the assumption that their mothering must have been deficient. Baba Yaga, as an ambiguous mother figure, gives us a different model for mothering which doesn't conform to the cultural norms of motherhood involving self-sacrifice and benevolence. Her style of mothering may more aptly be described as "tough love," which does not lend itself to easy judgment, especially because in Vasilisa's case, Baba Yaga's mothering style was effective in producing a fully individuated young woman.

These tales depict the dark aspects of growing up, which may include the death of a mother, cruelty by a stepmother, or even resentment that an overwhelmed mother expresses toward her children. Baba Yaga helps individuals own and integrate the dark aspects of these experiences and claim their own anger and aggressive impulses, which function to move them forward. Vasilisa is transformed by her time with Baba Yaga. She becomes able to utilize the dark force of her anger at her stepfamily, symbolized by the demonic light she carries from Baba Yaga, to destroy them. On a psychological level, their "destruction" may simply reflect her separating from them and getting on with her life. On a social level, their destruction brings about justice for Vasilisa, who escapes their dire oppression and is liberated into her own authentic life.

The tale of Vasilisa is similar to the fairy tale of Cinderella, who was made to serve her stepmother and stepsisters after her mother's death. In a short version of the story, Cinderella's fate was changed when she was rescued by a prince who retrieved the slipper she lost at the ball and fitted it on her foot. The story deprives Cinderella of her own agency and prescribes a traditional female role for her in marrying the prince and living "happily ever after." She forgives her stepsisters, displaying graciousness akin to that of the Eumenides. Vasilisa, by contrast, discovered her agency as a result of her foray into the dark forest with Baba Yaga. Working through her own aggressive impulses toward her stepfamily, she was able to separate from them and change the course of her life by herself, without reliance on a prince to save her. She took control of her own life by moving away, taking up a vocation, and eventually meeting a man who became her lover but not her savior.

Baba Yaga, capricious and unpredictable as she might seem, gives us the tools to connect to our dark side, integrate it, and use it for our own growth and liberation from forces that impede our forward movement as healthy, whole individuals. Baba Yaga helped empower Vasilisa in breaking the chains of her oppression, bringing about a just conclusion to her story. In much the same way that Baba Yaga helped Vasilisa come into her own, women today need to band together to help each other out. The patriarchy pits women against each other because it can control us better that way. We compete for men and jobs and vie to be the most beautiful, the best mother, etc. Instead of competing against each other, we need to join in solidarity to lift each other up and become truly empowered.

CHAPTER TWELVE

The Gender Pay Gap

"This fight, which began as my own, is now our fight."
— Lilly Ledbetter

Removing the gender pay gap—the difference in average wages between men and women—is an example of a feminist issue that all women can rally around to lift each other up. It is striking and unacceptable that, despite women's gains in educational levels in the U.S., the gender pay gap has not budged for two decades. The U.S. has a long way to go to achieve pay equity. According to the 2023 Global Gender Gap Index, it ranks number 43 out of 146 countries. The Pew Research Center reports that in 2023 women earned just 82% of what men earned. For Black women, it was 70 cents for every dollar a man earned, and for Latina women, it was 65 cents (Kochhar, 2023).

The Equal Pay Act of 1963, signed into law by President John Kennedy, made it illegal for employers to pay women less than men for substantially equal work. At the time, women were paid 59 cents for every dollar a man earned. The act helped some but did not close the wage gap. The Paycheck Fairness Act, first introduced in 1997, when women's earnings had increased to 75 cents on the dollar, would tighten the Equal Pay Act so that any differences in pay would have to be based on factors other than sex. Employers have used the "factors other than sex" defense to justify paying men more because of their previous salary levels or their better negotiating skills, factors that are patently embedded in sexist norms; employers have also cited the need to pay men more in order to lure them away from other jobs. The Paycheck Fairness Act would remove any such defenses as not bona fide job-related factors. The act has not passed, however, despite being introduced by Congress more than 20 times.

Congress did pass the Lilly Ledbetter Fair Pay Act of 2009, signed into law by President Obama. Ledbetter had been employed as a manager at Goodyear Tire for 20 years before discovering that she had been paid thousands of dollars less per year than men in the same position. She filed a sex discrimination suit against Goodyear and won. The case was reversed on appeal and eventually reached the Supreme Court, which ruled against her because she did not file the suit within 180 days of the discriminatory policy. The Lilly Ledbetter Act allowed women to sue whenever they discovered discrimination, not just within the first 180 days of the policy. Ledbetter never received restitution from Goodyear but said, "I'll be happy if the last thing they say about me after I die is that I made a difference" ("LillyLedbetter," 2024). She later wrote a memoir about her experience, became an activist for women's employment equality, and was inducted into the National Women's Hall of Fame.

One factor that helps to explain the long-standing gender pay gap is occupational segregation, which results from women occupying more gendered professions such as nursing, teaching, health care support, and other service positions that are considered suitable for women but pay less. This type of occupational segregation is horizontal, in that such positions are disproportionately filled by women.

Vertical segregation, on the other hand, refers to gender stratification within an occupation. For instance, even though women now make up half of law school graduates, they become partners in law firms in only about 20% of cases (Saraswati, 2021). In such cases, women are frequently held to a higher standard than men or experience backlash when they negotiate for more advanced positions with higher pay. The result is that for structural reasons, women have trouble breaking through the "glass ceiling," which limits their advancement.

But even when women manage to advance into high-level positions typically held by men, patriarchy erects structural barriers to their earning power. When women enter fields that are dominated by men, pay levels drop, whereas when men enter fields that primarily women occupy, pay levels increase. Researcher Jorgen Harris found that a 10% increase in women in a specific occupation results in an 8% decrease in men's salaries and a 7% decrease in women's salaries (Harris, 2022). One explanation is that when women participate in an occupation, society values it less, despite the fact that women have higher levels of education and equivalent amounts of work experience (Miller, 2016). Another cause is stratification within professions: Currently, women doctors make on average $2 million less than men over a 40-year career, in part because women tend to go into primary care, whereas men tend to become surgeons; the gap is higher in medicine than in computer science or engineering (Ghorayshi, A., 2021). I could not find any studies showing that male doctors' incomes fall when women enter the field.

Harvard professor Claudia Goldin won the Nobel Prize in Economics in 2023 for her work on the gender pay gap. She was the third woman to win the Nobel in economics but the first as a solo author. The award draws attention to the importance of this issue, not only for women in the workforce but also for the health of the economy as a result of greater labor force participation by women. Goldin's work underscores the need to take corrective action to close the gender pay gap for all women.

Previously, the wage gap for women has been explained by occupation and educational attainment (horizontal segregation). Goldin's research, on the other hand, reveals differences within occupations, not between them, with differences heightened within the highest paying occupations such as business, law, and medicine (vertical segregation). Goldin discovered that the wage gap occurs mostly between men and women in the same jobs, and it usually starts after the birth of the first child. "We're never going to have gender equity, or narrow the pay gap, until we have couple's equity," Goldin concludes (Smith, 2023).

Her work highlights the fact that having children puts women at a disadvantage in the workforce because the division of labor at home is still unequal. Because of the difficulty balancing work and home life, one member of a couple focuses on career and the other, most often the woman, does most of the work at home, especially in caring for children. Employers pay less after women have children because they assume they are less committed. Additionally, women with children often want more flexible work hours, which employers value less.

Women's family and caregiving responsibilities often lead them to take part-time positions, which pay less, or to drop out of the workforce temporarily, which jeopardizes their advancement when they return. Once this pattern is created, it's hard to break out of, especially because the woman loses the chance for advancement in her career. The result is that working women with children experience the "motherhood penalty"—their wages go down when they have children. Fathers, on the other hand, see an increase in wages, the "fatherhood bonus," because it is assumed by employers that they have more responsibility to provide for their families.

Goldin's research shows that women with children make less income than women without children because of reduced work hours, but men with children actually make more than men without children, a situation known as the "fatherhood premium." In these cases, women's losses are men's gains. In an interview with *USA Today* on the day after she received the Nobel, Goldin said, "Men are able to step forward because women step backward. It's not simply taking the shirts to the dry cleaners that women do; they are boosting their [men's] ability to do work. And therefore if you are by yourself [as a single man], you don't have the ability to have that helpmate" (Ramaswamy, 2013).

Goldin points to the 1970s as a period of progress for working women, primarily because of the availability of contraception, which enabled women to marry later and pursue educational goals leading to greater career opportunities. These opportunities did not, however, close the wage gap. Traditional gender roles, which call for women to have the bulk of childcare responsibilities, remain a block to closing the gap. Gender dynamics are slow to change, and although they have evolved since the '70s, they seem to be going backward now. With Roe being overturned, traditional roles may be returning, with women now being made to endure forced pregnancies. And with right-wing politicians calling for limitations on the availability of contraception, traditional gender roles may become even more entrenched. Conservative politicians and judges are sending women the message that their proper place is in the home—having babies and taking care of them. Lacking the freedom to make choices about their reproductive status, women will be hampered in entering the workforce and achieving pay equity with men.

Although "couple equity" is a worthy goal, legislation and public policy initiatives cannot directly affect how couples negotiate shared responsibilities; such policies can, however, create a backdrop of conditions that may influence equitable gender relations. Even though gender equality within a couple's relationship cannot be prescribed by society, that doesn't mean society is off the hook for creating conditions that could lead to more "couple equity." Hopefully Goldin's work, and the Nobel Prize she was awarded, will help to increase awareness of the changes that society needs to make to lessen the gender pay gap. Paid family leave can make a big difference in preventing women from dropping out of the workforce after children arrive, especially if their jobs are held for them during the paid leave. Universal childcare can also enable women to be full participants in the workforce by relieving them from the caretaking responsibilities that unfortunately still fall more heavily on them.

Adopting policies of family leave and universal childcare will provide structural supports that enable women to be more committed to their jobs, in turn decreasing employer bias against them. Another problem contributing to the pay gap is that women with children often want more flexible work hours, which employers value less. If women are relieved of the burden of providing the bulk of childcare through universal childcare, they may not need flexible working schedules that accommodate the needs of children. Of course, even if women do stay in the labor market, there is no guarantee that they will be paid equally, especially in professional careers where pay discrepancies are more marked.

Hopefully, Goldin's research and well-deserved award will help make employers aware that the pay inequities women face are a form of discrimination that can no longer be tolerated. Pay equity will likely attract more women to the labor market; everyone benefits from women's greater participation and from the multitude of talents and gifts that gender diversity provides—not just women themselves but also companies and the economy as a whole.

It isn't only women's disproportionate share of family responsibilities, however, that leads to the gender pay gap. Sexual harassment in the workplace also contributes to the gender pay gap by creating power imbalances that limit women's opportunities. Thirty-eight percent of women report sexual harassment in the workplace (hracuity, 2023). Unwanted sexual advances, requests for sexual favors in exchange for promotion, lewd comments, and the presence of pornography or offensive pictures all undermine women's participation in the workforce and limit their advancement. Women in hostile work environments may feel less empowered to negotiate promotions and pay increases. They may also become depressed or anxious, leading to poor job performance, increased rates of absenteeism, and early retirement. Sexual harassment is prohibited by Title VII of the Civil Rights Act of 1964 but remains a serious and widespread problem that is harmful to women in the workplace, especially those marginalized by race, class, and gender identity/sexual orientation. Women have every right to be angry about the limitations they face in the work world and the unfair advantage men have in advancement and remuneration. Feminists need to be persistent and strident in fighting for the dismantling of patriarchal structures that underlie the workplace environment. They must press for transparency of salary levels and benefits for various positions, which will help them negotiate fair levels of both. They must fight for the eradication of sexual harassment from the workplace, the elimination of discrimination against women based on stereotypical gender norms, and equal opportunities for advancement that will help women, finally, break through the glass ceiling. As Ledbetter said, "This fight, which began as my own, is now our fight" (Ledbetter).

That fight was taken up by the women of Iceland, who went on strike to protest the gender pay gap on October 24, 2023. Thousands of women from all occupations, from the Prime Minister, Katrin Jakobsdottir, to CEOs, teachers, and house cleaners, refrained from work, both paid and unpaid, to demand equal pay. The slogan of the strike was "You call this equality?" The last such strike was in 1975, when 90% of women walked away from work to demonstrate solidarity against pay discrimination. According to the World Economic Forum, Iceland has a gender wage parity of 90%, the highest of any nation, a record it has held for 14 years. Despite that high ranking, Icelandic women are committed to closing the pay gap completely.

When Freyja Steingrimsdottir, one of the organizers of the strike and communications director of the Icelandic Federation of Public Workers, was asked in an interview why the strike was called in one of the most progressive countries in the world, she replied:

> Since we're topping all these global indexes, there's been this … collective feeling for the women's rights movements in Iceland that we're not supposed to ask for any more. But what we say is … if we're going to be the global leaders in gender equality, then we should actually achieve it because it's possible … . If we're standing still, there's a possibility of a backlash, and we want to be going forward and not backward. So when there's still a way to go, we will fight for it (Summers, 2023).

Elise Gould, senior economist at the Economic Policy Institute, has suggested some ways to create more gender equality in the U.S. workforce, such as making health care more accessible, encouraging women to pursue professional careers in male-dominated fields, and promoting pay transparency.

But Goldin's work has shown that even these initiatives do not close the gender pay gap. Gould admits that there's no "one-size-fits all solution when gendered pay difference maps across so many different systems, especially race." She concludes that "there's no silver bullet in the United States to close the gender pay gap" because of the degree of economic inequality that exists, especially when race is factored in (Smith). Caregiving jobs are often filled by Black and Brown women who do not earn a living wage, especially if they are immigrants. Gender contributes to pay inequities, but the intersection of race and gender exacerbates the disparities.

The U.S. can learn from the Icelandic women who went on strike. If American women refrain from work for a day, the contribution they make to the economy, in both paid and unpaid work, will be highlighted. Much of women's work, especially in unpaid roles, is taken for granted. A strike would make their work visible and raise awareness about the need for equitable pay levels. If men are left to pick up the pieces when women walk out of work for a day, they may value women's work more and be more open to full wage equality. The same is true for companies which depend on women's work. Given the political climate in the U.S., however, it's unlikely that a strike would lead to unpaid work being remunerated, but a strike could be a first step in that direction. Because of the intersectional nature of the gender pay gap, American feminists need to form a multiracial, multiethnic coalition to combat pay inequities. A strike would perhaps be the strongest action they could take to bring about a just system of wage employment.

Marinette

Marinette

Art by Erika Busse.

Marinette is a fierce and destructive deity who is part of the indigenous Haitian pantheon which emerged during slavery. Deities who are part of this pantheon use ritual tools, such as whips and gunpowder, that had been wielded against them by slaveholders. Marinette is a goddess who can inspire women to demand equal compensation and recognition for their work.

Marinette, who was originally a priestess of the African-Haitian goddess Erzulie Danto, sacrificed a black pig in a Vodou ceremony and wrote a pact in its blood, which initiated the Haitian revolution. Afterward she became enshrined as a deity herself. However, she harbors rage against injustice as a result of not being celebrated as the force which started the Haitian revolution against France. She was pursued by the French but then banned from the battlefield by revolutionary leader Toussaint L'Ouverture, who was glorified instead. Marinette became frustrated at often being dismissed as an evil spirit while her male counterpart was honored. Many women today can relate to men taking credit for work they actually do.

Marinette is depicted as a bird with claws for hands and feet and eyes red with rage. She is considered a dangerous spirit who should not be invoked indoors because of her fiery nature; she is so hot with rage that her presence can cause the building to burst into flames, even unintentionally. She has been syncretized to Joan of Arc, and in Catholic art, she is pictured as Anima Sola, a chained woman burning in the fires of purgatory. Her animal companions are screech owls and loups-garou, or Haitian werewolves.

Marinette found herself working alone for justice from the French, just as Lilly Ledbetter did for equal pay. Although they both made significant progress working alone, we can be inspired by them to band together and make even greater progress.

CHAPTER THIRTEEN

"Women's Work"

"... none of us, including businesses, could do without the invisible, unpaid work that carers do."
— Caroline Criado Perez

Paid Maternity Leave

One of the biggest issues standing in the way of women's advancement is the lack of paid maternity leave. The Family and Medical Leave Act, passed in 1993, required companies of more than 50 employees to provide 12 weeks of unpaid leave and protect jobs during leave for childbirth, adoption, and family illness. But the FMLA did not do enough, as it does not apply to the entire workforce and does not provide equity between men and women in returning to work. The U.S. is the only member of the Organization for Economic Co-operation and Development, and one of only six countries in the world, that does not provide paid parental leave (bipartisanpolicy, 2022).

Women are disadvantaged by the absence of paid parental leave. As they are more likely to be the caregivers of children, they are more likely than fathers to leave the workforce after giving birth. A study funded by the March of Dimes and conducted by Institute for Women's Policy Research found that paid leave reduces the number of women dropping out of the workforce by 20% in the first year after giving birth and 50% after five years. Women are more likely to return to work if their job is held for them during paid leave, benefiting not only their own finances but also the economy as a whole. Paid leave also improves the health of mother and baby, improving mother-infant bonding and decreasing rates of neonatal and infant death (March of Dimes, 2020).

During Donald Trump's first term as president, his daughter Ivanka Trump campaigned for and ultimately persuaded her father to sign the Federal Employee Paid Leave Act, which guarantees 12 weeks of paid leave for certain federal employees under circumstances covered by FMLA. However, the act does not cover all federal employees and still leaves the majority of American working women without job protection and financial support while taking leave to care for children. Feminists must continue to fight for the right to paid leave, putting them on par with working women in other industrialized countries.

Universal Childcare

One of the reasons women are disadvantaged in the job arena is that despite having the majority of childcare duties, they do not have access to paid childcare, also known as universal childcare. During World War II, the federal government provided its first and only paid childcare to women who entered the workforce as a result of men fighting the war. The Lanham Act funded "war nurseries" that took care of children while women went to work to support the war effort, often working in war plants as "Rosie the Riveter." It was successful in providing high quality childcare, which enabled women to enter the workforce, but it was discontinued after the war.

As many as 75% of women, having a newfound sense of financial independence, wanted to continue to work after the war, but most were laid off (Khan Academy, 2024). Once again, men became the breadwinners, as women returned to the home and resumed childcare responsibilities. Conservative activist and anti-feminist Phyllis Schlafly advocated for the resumption of such traditional gender roles. She decried day care as "stranger care" and called for women to embrace their role as stay-at-home moms.

In 1971, Congress approved a bill to provide quality childcare to all families based on their ability to pay, but then-President Richard Nixon vetoed it on the grounds that it would destroy family life. Schlafly agreed, stating, "There's no real substitute for the care of the real mother" (leaving aside the question of what a "real" mother is, especially in cases of adoptive or foster mothers). And in 1989, when the Senate was considering the Dodd-Kennedy bill to provide day care to poor families, Schlafly wrote to Republican Senator Orrin Hatch, a sponsor of the bill: "The Dodd bill is unjust and discriminatory because it discriminates against women who take care of their own children and taxes them in order to subsidize those who use stranger care" (Elliott, J., 2011). She shamed women who utilized childcare to work for relying on "institutional care" rather than occupying their proper role as caretakers of their own children. It turns out that Schlafly herself was using nannies to take care of her children while she obtained a law degree and pursued her career as an activist, a little-known fact that exposes her own hypocrisy.

Despite the influence of conservatives such as Schlafly, Lyndon Johnson started the Head Start program in 1965 as part of his War on Poverty. Head Start provides federal funding to meet the educational, social, and health needs of preschool children from low-income families. Head Start serves children from ages three to five, and Early Head Start from birth to three. All eligible families below the poverty line receive free childcare as well as other child development services. Funding provides for center- and home-based childcare in licensed facilities.

Free childcare results in significant savings for families whose childcare costs are second only to rent or mortgage expenses. As mothers and children comprise the greatest poverty group in the U.S., mothers who have access to childcare have the opportunity to ameliorate their financial situation by working outside the home; they are also able to pursue their own educational goals, which can in turn lead to employment advantages.

The Department of Health and Human Services, which administers the program, reports gains for enrolled children: They are "more likely to graduate from high school and college" and to have "improved social, emotional, and behavioral development " (U.S. Department of Health and Human Services, 2024). Positive effects transfer across generations, with improved outcomes for second-generation children (Arundel, 2022). Significant gains for the economy occur as well; for every dollar spent on Head Start, society reaps nine dollars in benefits in the form of "increased earnings, employment, family stability, decreased welfare dependency, crime costs, grade repetition, and special education" (National Head Start Association, 2022). In addition to providing such economic benefits, Head Start has been successful in creating a brighter future for families, mothers, and children below the poverty level.

The question then arises about why such benefits should be limited to low-income families. Arguments for universal childcare include a positive economic impact on society as a whole as well as gains for the cognitive, social, and emotional growth of all children. Children in day care have more opportunities to develop social skills with peers in a structured setting. A study by Sorbonne University found that children enrolled in day care before the age of three were more social and better behaved, with effects lasting into adolescence. The author of the study, Maria Melchior, said, "Access to high-quality childcare in the first years of life may improve children's emotional and cognitive development, prevent later emotional difficulties and promote pro-social behaviors" (Haller, 2018). The social and emotional benefits of day care cannot be underestimated, as it gives young children the opportunity to learn about respect and equality between the sexes, thus helping to create an egalitarian society that promotes feminism.

In addition, universal childcare can operate as an economic driver by putting more parents, especially mothers, into the workforce, countering inflation by decreasing labor shortages and supporting childcare providers and early childhood educators, most of whom are women. Universal childcare would provide more employment opportunities for women in these professions.

From a human rights perspective, access to free childcare will enhance the empowerment of all women by enabling them to increase their earning power in the workforce and to pursue educational opportunities that promote their advancement in society. Women have rights to equal participation in the workforce, as well as equal opportunities to further their education, but the bulk of childcare responsibilities that currently falls on them interferes with realizing these rights. Only with access to free, high-quality childcare will women be able to achieve full equality with men. Feminists must continue to work for universal childcare so that they can be full participants in society with the same opportunities as men.

Unpaid Work

An issue related to universal childcare is the unpaid work of women, primarily in the areas of caring for children, elders and the sick—cooking, cleaning, chauffeuring, shopping, farming, fetching water, and gathering firewood. Such highly feminized work is not directly paid or remunerated. Globally, 75% of unpaid work is performed by women, whose unpaid work runs an average of three to six hours per day compared to 30 minutes to two hours for men (Perez). In the U.S., women spend 4.5 hours per day on unpaid work, whereas men spend 2.78 hours. If American women were reimbursed a minimum wage for their unpaid work, it would amount to approximately $1.5 trillion or 7% of the Gross Domestic Product (GDP), which measures the total value of goods and services in the economy. Similarly, in Argentina, unpaid work by women amounts to 7% of the GDP, whereas in Tanzania, a less developed country, it constitutes 63% (Perez).

It is important to include unpaid work by women in the GDP because it assigns value to such work, which is essential for society to function, highlights the benefits such work brings to the economy, and underscores the sacrifices many women make so that other family members are able to work or attend school. Surveys similar to those that track economic activity can help to calculate contributions made to the GDP by unpaid workers. The Organization for Economic Co-operation and Development (OECD) collects statistics on unpaid work by men and women in many countries, which can draw attention to gender inequalities.

Performing the bulk of unpaid work penalizes many women who are not able to enter the workforce because of their caregiving responsibilities, depriving them of good wages, pensions, and other benefits of employment, such as health insurance.

Some countries have taken steps to address the problem. In Uruguay, for example, care laws ensure that care is provided to all people in need, including children, the elderly, and the disabled. The state provides funding as well as training for such care programs; it has taken care out of the private sphere and elevated it to a human rights issue. This new model of care "is not only about providing certain services," says Julio Bango, National Secretary of Care in Uruguay; "it is part of a cultural battle, a policy to reduce gender inequalities" (UNWomen, 2017).

Other models include government funding of public works projects that have previously depended on unpaid work. In Uttar Pradesh, a province in northern India, the government is providing wage employment for rural men and women digging wells as part of the Mahatma Gandhi National Rural Employment Guarantee Act, which offers minimum wages for 100 days of guaranteed employment. In the 12 years of the program, women's wages are almost equal to those of men, and their standard of living has improved, especially in terms of access to food and education (Nandi, 2017).

Solutions to the problem of unpaid care work by women include redistribution of care work through provision of good quality public services that ensure care for all those who need it, thus freeing women to pursue employment and education, as well as changing social norms so that women and men are expected to share more equally in unpaid work. Perez gives a compelling exhortation to reshape society's structure and attitudes in ways that value women's work, both paid and unpaid:

> The world of work needs a wholesale redesign—of its regulations, of its equipment, of its culture—and this redesign must be led by data on female bodies and female lives. We have to start recognizing that the work women do is not an added extra, a bonus that we could do without: women's work, paid and unpaid, is the backbone of our society and our economy. It's about time we started valuing it (Perez).

Against Gender Essentialism

Even though childcare and unpaid labor fall mostly to women, gender disparity along these lines is not natural, even though our culture considers it to be. There is nothing natural or innate about women doing the bulk of domestic work, which is founded on gender essentialism, the notion that men and women have different innate natures which incline them to different pursuits. As feminist philosopher Elizabeth Grosz states in her 1995 publication *Space, time and perversion: essays on the politics of bodies*, essentialism "entails the belief that those characteristics defined as women's essence are shared in common by all women at all times. It implies a limit of the variations and possibilities of change, as it is not possible for a subject to act in a manner contrary to her essence. Her essence underlies all the apparent variations differentiating women from each other. Essentialism thus refers to the existence of fixed characteristics, given attributes, and ahistorical functions that limit the possibilities of change and thus of social reorganization" (Grosz, 1995).

Gender essentialism posits that women's nature is essentially different from men's in various ways. In his best-selling book *Men Are from Mars, Women Are from Venus,* John Gray builds a case for essential differences between the sexes (Gray, 2012). The differences, he believes, are so vast that they warrant describing men and women as living on different planets. For instance, one of the major differences is that men try to fix whatever is wrong with a relationship, whereas women merely want to talk about it.

Apart from the issue of who does domestic work and is naturally suited to it, the question arises about women's potential to harness rage and aggression in the fight against injustice. To answer this question, the issue of differences in temperament between men and women becomes critical. Temperament is considered to be biologically based, independent of learning and the social construction of gender. One problem in researching temperament is that learning and socialization start to occur shortly after birth, so studies that are done later in the developmental process may not be able to tease out differences between nature and nurture. To get around this problem, studies have looked at differences in fetal testosterone levels.

One study by Jennifer Connellan found that infant boys looked longer at mobiles than at her face, which led to the conclusion that boys are more innately geared to attend to things and girls to emotions. The study was, however, deeply flawed. Some babies were tested on their backs, others on their parents' laps. In addition, Connellan knew the sex of the baby she was observing, which may have led to experimenter expectancy bias. Given the methodological flaws, the study needs to be repeated with more controlled conditions (Fine, 2010).

Other studies that focused on unusually high fetal testosterone levels, called congenital adrenal hyperplasia, found that girls with this condition developed male external genitalia but did not differ in gendered play activities. Anne Fausto-Sterling, a professor at Brown who has done extensive research on gender differences, says the sexes don't fall into separate buckets but rather exist on a continuum: "Men and women may be different, but only in the same way that every individual is from the next" (Fausto-Sterling, 1985). Since social conditioning begins at birth, much research that supports gender essentialism is flawed, while the little research that has been done under proper controls does not support gender essentialism.

CHAPTER FOURTEEN

Women Warriors

"I am woman, hear me roar."
— Helen Reddy

The existence of women warriors throughout history and the prevalence of fierce warrior goddesses from cultures around the world provide a strong counterargument against gender essentialism. Historically, there are examples of groups of women like the Amazons who, like the Gulaab Gang in India today, have become warriors. Until recently, the Amazons were considered a fantasy of Greek mythology—a group of lesbians who fought Hercules and cut off their right breasts so they could better utilize bows and arrows. Homer wrote about them in the *Iliad*, and they later became the prototype of Wonder Woman. Some historians have postulated that these warriors were actually beardless men mistaken for women.

But a 2019 excavation showed that the Amazons were a real-life group of Scythian women warriors of Persian descent from the Russian steppes some 2,500 years ago, right in the area where the Greeks thought they lived. A team from the Institute of Archaeology at the Russian Academy of Sciences discovered a grave with four female skeletons buried with arrowheads, spears, and horseback-riding gear. The women ranged in age from 12 to 50, more or less. "Amazons were long considered a myth. These discoveries show warrior women were real," said *The Washington Post* (Hawkins, 2019).

The assumption that any burial site where weapons are found must contain the remains of men has now been debunked. Recent analyses using DNA and bioarchaeology indicate that about a third of the graves of armed Scythian warriors belonged to women, who were trained to fight and engaged in combat.

Women from many cultures and time periods have been warriors. Adrienne Mayor, a scholar at Stanford who runs the Facebook page Amazons Ancient and Modern, points to many historical warrior women, including Cynane, half-sister to Alexander the Great, who learned the same military skills as her brother; the Arab queen Zenobia, who rebelled against Rome and conquered a third of the Roman Empire; and Joan of Arc, the most famous warrior woman in Europe. Joan of Arc was one of the fiercest warriors of all time, acting on her own inner guidance (which she attributed to archangels but might very well have been a warrior archetype living in her shadow) to lead the French to victory against the English. She was later burned at the stake, not an uncommon fate for women who renounced typical gender roles.

Another historical case of women warriors was portrayed in the movie *The Woman King*. The actress Viola Davis starred as the leader of a band of female fighters known as the Agojie, who protected the Dahomey tribe of West Africa from the 17th to 19th centuries. The film features fictionalized characters based loosely on historical records. There was in fact a uniformed fighting unit of women, but it's unclear whether, as the movie depicts, the Agojie fought the neighboring Oya tribe in Nigeria to stop the slave trade in favor of an economy based on palm oil.

What is not in dispute is the fierceness of these women warriors; a missionary who witnessed their fighting commented that they were "the scourge and terror of the whole surrounding country, always at war and generally victorious" (Solly, 2022). Historian Lynne Ellsworth Larsen notes that the ferocity of the Agojie challenged notions of the French about gender roles and led to the French characterizing the warrior roles of the Agojie as uncivilized, in need of the civilizing influence of colonization (Solly).

Dahomey's "Amazon" warriors, along with the Scythian Amazons, show that women are just as equipped as men to be courageous fighters; they refute gender stereotypes about women as passive and accommodating, unlike men, who are traditionally seen as aggressive and pugnacious. There is no suggestion in the history of either of these Amazonian tribes that they were merely imitating men, as they formed independent fighting units with their own leadership. The historical record of these female fighting troops is a counterexample to the generally assumed differences between the essential natures of men and women.

Iranian women today are demonstrating how fiercely women can fight in their protests against the morality police after the death of 22-year-old Mahsa Amini, who died while in police custody after being arrested for improper wearing of her hijab. The Iranian regime enforces a strict dress code for women and sends them to "reeducation" centers as punishment for their violations. Women are now rebelling against the repressive regime and have taken to the streets, burning their hijabs and cutting their hair. They are risking their lives, and in many cases have lost their lives or fled to other countries to escape persecution. Over 500 people have died, many of them men in the women-led protests, according to the U.S.-based Human

Rights Activists News Agency, although some estimates put the number much higher. The actions of Iranian women have created a women-led revolution.

Throughout Iranian culture and history, women have cut their hair as a sign of mourning as well as to protest against injustice. In *Shahnameh*, a 1,000-year-old Persian epic poem that is embedded in the culture of Iran, women cutting their hair is referred to as a sign of mourning. The poem tells the story of the killing of the hero Siyavash, whose wife and the women accompanying her cut their hair as a protest against the injustice. "Women cutting their hair is an ancient Persian tradition … when the fury is stronger than the power of the oppressor," tweeted Wales-based writer and translator Shara Atashi. "The moment we have been waiting for has come. Politics fueled by poetry" (Atashi, 2022). The characters in the poem have become part of the everyday culture of Iran as symbols and archetypes, she says.

Iranians consider hair to be a sign of beauty, although women are required to keep it hidden under their headscarves. "We want to show them that we don't care about their standards, their definition of beauty or what they think that we should look like," said 36-year-old Faezeh Afshan, an Iranian chemical engineer living in Bologna, Italy, who was filmed shaving off her hair. "It is to show that we are angry" (Alkhaldi & Ebrahim, 2022).

Iranian women have tapped into the power of their anger and rage against the long-standing oppression they have lived under, especially since the takeover by the Ayatollah Khomeini in 1979 that established the Islamic Republic. The rage they are experiencing has taken the form of a culturally driven means of expression through cutting hair, but it is no less powerful as a result.

Women are also expressing their rage in the more direct and less culturally sanctioned action of burning their hijabs. Fire is often used as a symbol of passionate zeal that erupts after it can no longer be contained through cultural means, destroying anything that lies in its path. The burning of hijabs becomes a potent and dramatic way for women to destroy a symbol of their oppression.

The protests in Iran have galvanized support around the globe for Iranian women's rights and freedom, with solidarity events taking place across the U.S. and in many other countries, including Turkey, Germany, and Italy. In the U.K., British-Iranian women marched in London on International Women's Day in 2023. They wore red cloaks and white bonnets, invoking costumes from *The Handmaid's Tale*.

Anahita

The ferocity of Iranian women today may have its roots in the history, myths, and religion of ancient Iran, known as Persia. A deity of the old pre-Islamic religion, Anahita, who was the goddess of fertility, water, and war, was worshipped widely in Persia. She was depicted as a beautiful woman wearing a white, gold-embroidered robe and gold earrings, necklace, and crown. She held ritual twigs, symbolizing the vegetable kingdom and its fertility, and drove a four-horse chariot across the sky. She was celebrated in rituals that began with the fire of the creator god Ahura Mazda and concluded with quenching water provided by Anahita.

She was worshipped in more temples and shrines than any other Persian deity, including Mithras, the sun god, and was even considered more important than Ahura Mazda. Kings, wanting to please her as the goddess of war, sent the heads of their conquered enemies to her shrines for display. In the first

Anahita
Art by Erika Busse.

century C.E., her shrines became Zoroastrian temples, but she continues to be honored by the Zoroastrian faith today. Modern-day visitors to her temples still touch her waters in the hope that their prayers will be answered.

The Persian Empire fell to the Arab Muslims in 651 C.E., after which the worship of Anahita was suppressed. She morphed into Bibi Shahrbanu, "Lady of the Land," the widow of the Muslim hero and martyr Husayn ibi Ali, grandson of the prophet Muhammed and third Shi'a imam.[5] Thereafter, Anahita's temples became associated with Shahrbanu and remain so today, especially the temple at Shah-e Ray in the Tehran province of Iran. Shahrbanu provides an important link between pre-Islamic Persia and modern Shi'ism (a sect of Islam). Legend says that after Husayn was defeated in battle, he gave her his horse and bade her to flee back to her homeland in Persia. Pursued by Husayn's enemies, she came upon a mountain which trapped her. She called out "Oh mountain," whereupon the mountain miraculously opened and enveloped her in safety, but a piece of her veil got caught and left behind as she entered. It became an object of veneration, and a shrine was built on its site, still standing in a suburb of Tehran.

It's hard to know whether the history, religion, and legend of Anahita/Shahrbanu have influenced Iranian women in their current protests against the oppressive theocratic regime in Iran. However, a fierce goddess of war such as Anahita may very well live in the depths of their psyches as part of their cultural and psychic inheritance.

---

[5] The suppression of the older goddess Anahita by a patriarchal religion parallels the way Christianity coopted the ancient goddess Isis into the form of the Black Madonna.

Records from ancient Greece reveal that Persia also produced warrior women—Amazons who, dressed in Persian clothing, fought against the Greeks (Shokoohi, 2021). And Persian warrior woman Pantea Arteshbod was a commander who maintained law and order during the reign of Cyrus the Great, 559-530 B.C.E., (Shokoohi). This warrior woman heritage is perhaps a substrate of the psyches of the revolutionary Iranian women who today are fighting for "Woman, Life, Freedom."

American feminists, in their fight for equality, can learn from Iranian women, whose moral outrage against the oppressive regime in Iran has ignited their protests. The fury of Iranian women has fueled their movement for liberation. And although American feminists will not be risking their lives in protests against a totalitarian and repressive regime (not yet), they can nevertheless tap into the rage of Iranian protesters, using it as fuel to motivate their own fight against injustice. Iranian women are joining Black and Brown feminists around the world waging a fight against injustice, and their protests highlight the need for an intersectional global movement in which women of all races and ethnicities unite to throw off patriarchy.

In her podcast "Feminist Giant," Mona Eltahawy says, "As you watch the glory and power of the feminist revolution against theocrats in Iran, ask yourself where the fuck is your feminist revolution against theocrats in the U.S." She goes on to say: "Next time you are tempted to ask how it got so bad for women in Iran, ask yourself how you allowed white, Christian zealots to use democracy to cut it at its knees by destroying the right to abortion—a right which most Americans support. And recognize that the destruction of that right is but the first of many other destructions. Anyone who is not an able-bodied, white, cisgender, heterosexual man should fear what is to come."

She concludes by asking, "Where is your fucking rage? Where is your feminist revolution against your theocrats?" (Eltahawy, 2022). She concludes that it's easier for American feminists to criticize the patriarchal regime in Iran and valorize the women who are fighting it there, without looking at the patriarchal abuses of our own system and mobilizing our own rage against them.

Where is our rage against our own theocracy that polices what we do with our own bodies?

Historically, women warriors from around the world, as well as fierce goddesses from many different cultures, such as Anahita, offer examples of a fighting spirit that can motivate women to take action against injustice and reinvigorate the feminist movement.

Oya

Shutterstock standard image licensed.
https://www.shutterstock.com/image-generated/
oya-goddess-storms-sky-summoning-tornado-2418211423.

CHAPTER FIFTEEN

Warrior Goddesses

"Now I'm a warrior. I've got thicker skin.
I'm a warrior. I'm stronger than I've ever been."
— Demi Lovato

Oya

Oya, a West African Yoruba goddess, is a classic warrior goddess known for her courage in battle. Her ardent demeanor provides a classic case against gender essentialism and can motivate women to fight for equality with men. She is a dark goddess still worshipped today in Africa, with offerings of bean cakes made to her. Depicted with spiky hair, Oya holds a sword in one hand to cut through obstacles and a horsetail whip in the other hand to control powerful wind and storms. A beaded veil covers her face, much like a mask, and she twirls the rainbow skirt she wears. Oya is known as the Mother of Nine because, after giving birth to stillborn babies, she made an offering of rainbow-colored material to the supreme god Olorun and afterward gave birth to nine children—four sets of twins and a single child. Nine became her sacred number, and she's often depicted with nine whirlwinds swirling around her. She is regarded as the protector of women, who call on her to resolve conflicts.

Oya was the daughter of Obatala, god of creation, and favorite wife of Shango, god of thunder and lightning. Together they are a fearsome couple, not to be messed with. Shango had two wives, Oshun and Oba, when he first spotted Oya in the marketplace. Thinking her the most beautiful woman he had ever seen, he wanted her to be his third wife. His oracle told him to approach her carefully because of her great power and fierce temper. He discovered that she could shapeshift into an antelope by putting on its skin, which she hid when she transformed into a woman. He tricked her by stealing the skin and offering to give it back to her if she married him, which she agreed to do. (This story is reminiscent of the Celtic tale of a Selkie who lives as a seal but changes into a woman and finds her sealskin stolen by a suitor.)

Oya became Shango's partner in battle. He trusted her and asked her for assistance in defeating his enemies. Once, when he was outnumbered by his enemies and lacking food, soldiers, or a horse, he turned to Oya. She concocted a plan which involved the two of them exchanging clothes and even hair. Shango shaved his beard and gave it to Oya, who came to be known as "she who grows a beard in war." Shango, attired in one of Oya's dresses as a disguise, made it past enemy lines and defeated his opponents. This story illustrates that Oya was fluidly able to take on masculine characteristics and, like many fierce goddesses, balance masculine and feminine energies.

Shango's powers synchronized well with Oya's. Shango was the proud owner of thunderstorms, and when Oya would set the wind in motion, he would follow with thunder and lightning. She often cleared out deadwood with her wind, but sometimes, when she was angry at the injustices committed by humans, she used her wind to wipe out whole villages. Oya became Shango's favorite wife, and she stayed with him through troubles that caused his first two wives to leave him.

Another story which highlights Oya's destructive nature has to do with assistance Oya gave Orunmila, an orisha (or deity) of divination who was constantly doing battle with his enemies. He called on several orishas for help to no avail. Finally, he sought out Oya, who asked for a basket and two hens as payment for her work. She assured him that his problem would be solved by the next day. Orunmila went to sleep, and when he awoke the next day, he discovered that a tornado had hit in the night and wiped out the whole village. Shocked, he reproached her for killing all his enemies, when he just wanted them to leave him alone. She replied that he was too softhearted, as his enemies would constantly pursue him with no reprieve. She had solved his problem and asked for her payment, deal concluded.

Like many other dark goddesses, Oya stands for wiping away the old, dead things that no longer serve us in order to make room for the new. As the goddess of wind, Oya has the power to destroy, much as hurricanes and tornadoes ravage landscapes and the people who occupy them. But she also brings about change and transformation with her destructive powers. She defeats the limiting power of the ego with her sword (much like Kali, symbolized by the severed head she holds) to create a greater, more expansive experience of life. Oya vanquishes the false self of the ego to allow a new, more authentic self to emerge. As she clears away dead wood, new trees can grow. Her creative powers bring rain to areas devastated by drought, restoring abundance by helping crops grow.

Oya is a goddess of transitions, calming those who are afraid of death by aiding in their transition from life to death. If she realizes that someone on the edge of death still has unfinished business with life, she can stop the transition and send them back to complete their work. Her relationship with death makes her the guardian of graveyards. She is a supremely powerful goddess, embodying aspects of death as well as life.

Oya has stood the test of time, not only because she is still worshipped in Africa but also because she has morphed into a popular mutant superhero figure in Marvel comic books. As a superhero she has retained her power to change the weather, especially through temperature manipulation. And as one of the X-Men, she is battle-worthy. When she attends an opening of the Mutant History Museum (San Francisco Museum of Mutant History, 2011), she finds herself in the midst of an attempt to plant a bomb in it by members of the Hellfire Club. She murders them all and expresses no regret. With her superpowers, she does what is necessary to preserve the right order of society. It is not surprising that she has survived over the centuries, even becoming a superhero in Western culture, as she represents the fierce, powerful, and heroic nature of womankind across all cultures and all time.

The Morrigan

In Celtic mythology, the Morrigan, or Morrigu, is the goddess of war, fate, and prophecy. The Morrigan is not actually her name but rather a title meaning “Phantom Queen,” “Nightmare Queen,” or “Great Queen.” Sometimes the Morrigan is referred to as a single goddess whose name is Anu, and at other times she is described as a triple goddess consisting of three sisters—Macha, Badb, and Anu. All three are goddesses of war, each with her own personality and attributes, but when the Morrigan is mentioned as a single goddess, the reference is usually to Anu.

All three goddesses belong to the Tuatha dé Danann, indigenous inhabitants of Ireland who were later mythologized

The Morrigan

Art by Cynthia A. Morgan. "Morrigan - Goddess of War".

as gods or demigods descended from the sky. Because most of the Irish traditions were kept alive orally, before written records of the Christian era, it's impossible to know whether the Tuatha dé, including the Morrigan, were actual historical people or merely mythological figures. The Morrigan is, however, a strictly Irish goddess, whereas many other Celtic deities originated from European countries such as France, Spain, and the British Isles.

The Morrigan is in that sense a place-based goddess, identified with the natural world in Ireland, although she is not limited to a specific geological feature, as some land-based goddesses are. As a representation of nature, she can be either benevolent or destructive, depending on weather and other natural phenomena.

The Tuatha dé were a race of short, dark people who were eventually defeated around 1000 B.C.E. by the Milesians—Gaels who settled in Ireland after migrating from Iberia and became the ancestors of today's Irish people. The Tuatha dé then retreated into the land of the sídhe, or fairy world. The Morrigan, whether as a fairy or mythological being, was kept alive and worshipped by the Irish people, even after the Tuatha dé were defeated. She took refuge in the Cave of the Cats (called Oweynagab in Irish), a muddy limestone cave that was considered Ireland's gate to hell, an entrance to the Otherworld. Monsters and spirits were said to live there and made howls that sounded like the cries of cats. Like Hecate, the Morrigan lived in a cave, a habitation somewhere between the Underworld and the world above ground, a liminal space between the two worlds.

In Irish folklore, the Morrigan emerged from the cave every Samhain eve (the start of the Celtic new year, when the veil between the worlds is thin) on a one-legged horse drawing a chariot. She is reputed to be a bean sídhe, or a banshee[6] of the fairy folk. Her reputation as a banshee seems to derive from her power to deliver death omens. She embodies the washer who announces a death by washing the person's bloody clothes or armor in a river, often wailing or screaming, much as the "cats" in her cave. Whenever the banshee cries, a death is close at hand.

The Morrigan has been described as a red-haired woman with red eyebrows seated on a chariot, wearing a red cloak that drags behind her. As a goddess of war and an instigator of battle, she is associated with the color red because it is the color of blood. As a goddess of war and death, she is violent and bloodthirsty, but her victories in battle create the opportunity for something new to be created. She is celebrated as a hero on the battlefield, defending against the powers that threaten the Tuatha dé. As the daughter of the fertility goddess Ernmas and the sorcerer god Cailitin, she comes by her powers naturally.

Like many fierce goddesses, the Morrigan is a shapeshifter who takes the form of different animals, most commonly crows or ravens. These birds were symbols of war and prophecy, appearing after battles to feed on the carrion. The Irish considered crows and ravens to be birds of omens, specifically harbingers of death. They also saw them as psychopomps, carrying dead souls into the Otherworld. The Morrigan's identification with ravens and crows led to her association with the color black. Morgan Le Fay of Arthurian legend was also a fairy and a shapeshifter associated with the raven, which led some writers to allege she was the Morrigan, but there is no historical basis for that connection (Weber, 2019).

---

[6] A banshee is a female spirit who wails whenever a family member dies or is near death.

The Tuatha dé, led by the Morrigan, fought the Fir Bolg, a people who originated in Ireland but returned after settling in Greece for 200 years. After defeating the Fir Bolg at the first battle of Cath Maige Tuired, the Tuatha dé fought the mythical, evil Femorians, aided by the god Lugh, whose fighting skills were solicited by the Morrigan. The groundwork for the second battle of Cath Maige Tuired against the Femorians was laid by the Morrigan's relationship with the god Dagda, chief of the Tuatha dé. About a year before the battle, he had arranged to meet the Morrigan at Samhain. He found her straddling a river, one foot on each bank, washing her genitals while nine plaits of her hair hung loose. They consummated their relationship there, and the place was afterward known as "the bed of the couple." After their union, the Morrigan asked him to gather skilled fighters, and together they routed the Femorians.

In the story Táin Bó Cúailnge, the national epic of Ireland, also known as the Cattle Raid of Cooley, the provinces of Ulster and Connacht battled each other. The warriors from Connacht were intent on stealing the potent bull of Cooley known as Donn Cuailnge. The men of Ulster were incapacitated by an illness, leaving 17-year-old Cú Chulainn to defend them. The Morrigan engaged him in battle, shapeshifting sequentially into a slippery eel, a wolf, and then a red heifer leading a stampede. He tried to dominate her with patriarchal one-upmanship, telling her she will not be healed from her injuries on the battlefield until he blesses her.

She then appeared to him as an old woman milking a cow. He begged her for some milk, and she showed herself to be benevolent, and spiritually more powerful, by obliging. Not recognizing her, he blessed her, and all her injuries were healed. The next day as he prepared to fight in a battle, several bad omens occurred. His horse, refusing to be harnessed, wept tears of blood.

And he passed the Morrigan washing bloody clothes in a river; he asked whose clothes she was washing, and she replied they were his. During the fighting, Cu Chulainn was disemboweled. Holding his guts, he went to a nearby lake to wash himself and prepare for death. He spotted a stone pillar and tied himself to it with his entrails so he would die standing up. The Morrigan, shapeshifting into a crow, perched on the pillar, and, victorious, signaled his death.

As reflected in the story of Cu Chulainn, the Morrigan is associated with cattle and cattle raids. The Irish were a cattle culture that depended on cows for currency, clothing, and food in the form of milk and meat. Milk was prized as life-giving and healing, as evidenced in the tale of Cu Chulainn. The survival of cattle was a life-or-death matter for the Irish. If herds of cows were reduced by poor weather or disease, the people faced ill health or starvation. The Morrigan's connection to cattle made her a crucial goddess to petition for plentiful food and drink. Cattle raids were an important part of warfare between clans to ensure adequate food supplies, especially during harsh winters. "Stealing cows was important in this society," says archaeologist Daniel Curley of the National University Ireland Galway. "It was a ready source of wealth, a slight to opponents' honor and power, and a pseudo-martial sport" (*Archaeology Magazine,* 2022).

The Morrigan demonstrates the power of cattle when she leads a stampede as a heifer against Cu Chulainn. She is a goddess the Irish people can relate to, as she reflects their everyday concerns and activities related to survival and power. They understand her as a figure who is a divinity but at the same time one of them. The Morrigan may seem ruthless at times, but she does not shirk from taking to the battlefield when duty, honor, or survival require it. She can inspire women today to fight for what they need and believe in, even in a patriarchal society that does not support their empowerment.

The Morrigan did not adhere to the norms for Irish women at the time, whose rights were inferior to men's. Women were considered to be legally incompetent, equal to children and slaves. Daughters could inherit an interest in land if they had no brothers but could not legally own or bequeath it. Men, unlike women, could have more than one spouse, and their grounds for divorce were much greater, including abortion, infertility, infidelity, and laziness in housekeeping, whereas women could divorce only in cases of homosexuality, physical abuse, or impotence (Weber).[7]

It is surprising that the Morrigan, as such a fierce and powerful goddess, could arise in a culture that was not supportive of women's rights. She challenges the authority of men by standing in her power. She engages in stereotypically male activities such as war and cattle raids but never wields a weapon, nor does she need to; her powers are magical and resemble the forces of nature. She inspires women to speak truth to power and fight for their beliefs. In this sense the Morrigan is primarily a goddess of empowerment who pushes women to meet challenges in their lives, regardless of the gender bias of the society in which they live. Her voice encourages women to fight for their own freedom and not be cowed by men, so to speak. As a dark goddess, she serves as a model for women to

---

[7] The situation of women's rights in Ireland has improved dramatically. Today reproductive rights include the right to abortion until 12 weeks of pregnancy, subject to a three-day waiting period, passed into law in 2018, as well as the right to contraception, granted in 1985; Ireland was the last country in the West to legalize contraceptives, undoubtedly because of the influence of the Catholic Church. Divorce was made legal for women in 1996, and the right to 26 weeks of paid maternity leave was passed in 1994. Many challenges remain, however, especially in terms of the gender pay gap and violence against women; the European Union's Gender Equality Strategy, which includes Ireland, will hopefully bring full equality to women.

explore the darkness and find their way through it without fear (Weber).

I find it curious that in a patriarchal society such as Celtic Ireland, the deity who inspired men to fight was female. Some Celtic women were warriors, such as the Celtic queen Medb, but most women were spectators to battles. My sense is that the Morrigan, as a chthonic, or Underworld, goddess, had war powers derived from the land with which she was identified, a power no male deity could claim.

The fact that the Morrigan engaged in cattle raids points to her consolidation of power through securing herds of land animals. "The silent, omnipresent land goddess decided whether people would thrive or starve," explains Weber. "The task of the mortal people was to figure out how to be in relationship with such a presence" (Weber). As a land goddess, the Morrigan ruled over sovereignty, understood as controlling regions of land. The notion of sovereignty she represents is frequently misunderstood as reflecting autonomy of the individual self rather than authority over a region; the latter is more aligned with her battle-worthy nature that fights for control over areas of land.

The land in Ireland was always considered to be female. As Weber points out, "For the Celts, the land was life, pulsing with potential but also mystery and danger, one in which faeries lurked, one that could sometimes be a formidable enemy. … The land itself was a queen—the Great Queen" (Weber). As a goddess identified with the land, the Morrigan reminds us of the association often made between women and the land or the earth. Fierce goddesses such as the Morrigan embody the power and strength of the land, which is important to remember, as the earth is in danger and needs all the protection we can give it. In honoring the Morrigan, we also honor the earth and take action to save it.

CHAPTER SIXTEEN

Enraged Earth

"I'm not a patriot to a flag, I'm patriot to a land."
—Winona LaDuke

Many fierce goddesses are universal goddesses like Kali, whose roots are from a particular culture but are not tied to a specific parcel of land or geographic feature. Such universal goddesses tend to be worshipped in many cultures and countries because, although they emerged from a given culture, they are not rooted in a particular land or water feature, making them more "portable" goddesses, as it were. Other fierce goddesses are tied to specific parcels of land or particular geographic features. They can be protectors of the people who inhabit the land as well as the land itself.

For example, many Celtic goddesses arose from the land or bodies of water and are thus land- or water-specific goddesses whose primary influence is felt in the area of land or water in which they are embedded. For instance, the Celtic goddess Bounn presides over the River Boyne in Ireland. And Danu is a local goddess of two mountains in Kerry, which are called "Danu's boobs."

A story about the war goddess Brigit, daughter of the Morrigan (from whom she inherited her pugnacious nature), describes how she came to inhabit land in Kildare, where later, after being coopted by Christianity, she built her monastery. She asked the King of Leinster for land which was suitable for her purposes, as it was near a forest containing firewood and berries and a lake for drinking water. The king, thinking that her request was laughable, declined. Undaunted, she asked for as much land as her cloak would cover. The king, still thinking her request was ridiculous and would come to nothing, agreed. Brigit then asked four of her sisters to grab ahold of the four corners of her cloak and run with them toward the four directions, respectively. As they did, the cloak magically expanded and covered the whole of the king's province. Frightened, the king succumbed to Brigit, who informed him that she was punishing him for his lack of generosity to poor people. A compromise was struck, in which he granted her a favorable plot of land, on which she built her pagan sanctuary, which later became an abbey.

Pele

The Hawaiian goddess Pele falls into the camp of goddesses who literally embody a piece of land, a geographic feature, or a body of water. Pele, a brown-skinned goddess who spews fire when her volcanic nature erupts, is believed to live in the lava pit of the active volcano Kilauea on the big island of Hawaii. When she is angered, she causes the volcano to erupt. Kilauea last erupted in September 2023, apparently when her anger overflowed. The effect was to reshape the landscape, destroying towns and vegetation but at the same time creating fertile new land. Pele becomes emblematic of the power to destroy the old while simultaneously creating a new, life-giving model.

Pele

Art by Allie McCormack. Pele the Volcano Goddess 2
https://www.deviantart.com/alliemccormack/art/
Pele-the-Volcano-Goddess-2-1059347251.

Pele lives in the crater of Kilauea, but she did not originate there. One of her myths tells the story of how she migrated there from Tahiti, the original site of the gods and homeland of the ancestors. Some scholars hypothesize that Pele's family were actual historical figures, perhaps Samoans who migrated to the Hawaiian Islands sometime between 100 and 800 C.E. and settled in the volcano region. Pele's parents, thought to be her mother, Haumea, and her father, Kane, were the original Hawaiian creator gods. Pele had a number of siblings, ranging from five sisters and seven brothers in one account (Reichard, 2015) to 61 sisters and 61 brothers (Nimmo, 2011); the latter numbers may be attributable to cousins considered as siblings.

En route from Tahiti in canoes, Pele and her siblings stopped on the island of Kauai, where Pele fell in love with Lohiau, the island's chief. Pele's jealous sister, the Sea Goddess, chased her as she traveled and tore her body apart in a huge battle on the island of Maui, where Pele's bones created a special land formation. Pele's spirit arose from the bones, and she became an immortal goddess, after which she continued her travels to the island of Hawaii, where she made her home in the crater of Kilauea.

Another well-known myth concerns Pele and her youngest sibling, Hi'iaka, whom Pele carried with her in an egg as she traveled from Tahiti. Once Pele settled on the volcano, her sister emerged from the egg and became a beautiful woman imbued with supernatural powers superseded only by Pele's. Longing for her lover Lohiau, Pele asked her sister to watch over her body while she went on a dreamtime journey to visit him. They made passionate love for three days, but when Pele left to rejoin her sleeping body, Lohiau was devastated and hanged himself.

Meanwhile Pele, unaware of his demise, asked her sister to travel to Kauai and bring him to her within 40 days. She was not keen to send Hi'iaka to retrieve him, for fear Lohiau might be attracted to her. So she exacted a promise from her sister that she would not encourage him in any way. And Hi'iaka was not eager to make the journey either, as she preferred to stay within her sacred groves and dance the hula with her friend Hopoe. She exacted a promise from Pele not to harm her groves or her friend while she was on her mission.

It took 40 days just for Hi'iaka to reach Kauai, and as she arrived, Lohiau's spirit was leaving his body. Hi'aka sang a powerful chant and pushed his spirit back into his body through his eye socket. The two of them departed for the island of Hawaii, where Pele awaited them. On the journey, Lohiau became attracted to Hi'aka and performed a passionate dance to woo her, but she remained faithful to her sister.

Pele, in a jealous rage because her sister had not returned in 40 days and fearing the two of them had become lovers, destroyed her sister's sacred groves and her friend in a volcanic eruption. Once Hi'iaka and Lohiau reached the big island of Hawaii, they found the area blackened by lava, and Hi'aka realized that Pele had betrayed her. As revenge, she embraced Lohiau in front of her sister. Pele retaliated with more lava, and Lohiau was killed, although Hi'aka was not hurt because she had the supernatural powers of a goddess. A brother of Pele was traveling by canoe from Tahiti and sighted Lohiau's spirit floating over the water on his return to his ancestral homeland. He rescued Lohiau's spirit and brought it back to Hawaii, where he infused it back into his body. Lohiau and Hi'aka were reunited and returned to Kauai together.

The story of Pele and her sister Hi'aka illustrates how common it is for women to compete for men with each other out of jealousy and envy. Instead of standing by each other and supporting each other, they turn against each other or, even worse, seek revenge. Pele demonstrated a caring demeanor toward her sister by carrying her from Tahiti in an egg, almost as if she were pregnant with her. But despite that, she betrayed her sister and destroyed her sacred groves. Even these two sisters, who shared a close family connection, could not maintain their sisterly connection and instead devolved into alienation and aggression. The same is true of the story of Pele and her sister the Sea Goddess, who tore Pele's body apart in an act of jealousy. In order to move feminism forward, women need to unite, form solidarity, and value their relationships with each other as much as with men. Pele's brother becomes the hero in the story, rescuing another man; in a patriarchal society men have a loyalty to each other, while patriarchy drives women apart.

Pele was known to have a number of lovers, but the most popular story about her love affairs described a rocky relationship with the pig-god Kamapua'a, who lived on Oahu but traveled among the Hawaiian islands, sometimes in pig form and sometimes in human form. Kamapua'a was a womanizer who got into trouble with the husbands of many of his conquests. He was what we would today call a male chauvinist pig. Kamapua'a was the opposite of Pele, preferring cool, damp environments rich with vegetation common on the windward side of the islands where waterfalls abound.

One day when Pele and her sister Kapo were out walking on Oahu, Kamapua'a caught sight of them and, overcome with desire, pursued Pele. Luckily, Kapo had a detachable vagina, which she threw in the opposite direction to distract Kamapua'a. Today on the island of Oahu there is a hill named Kohelepelepe (which means detached vagina) bearing the marks of the one Kapo threw. Kamapua'a, still in ardent pursuit of Pele, ventured onto Kilauea and entreated Pele to be his lover. She scorned him, calling him a pig and a son of a pig, among other epithets. A violent battle ensued, in which she threw fire and lava at him, chasing him into the sea, whereupon he shapeshifted into a fish. He drove heavy rainstorms onto her, which almost put out her fire. When Pele's brothers realized that her fires might be extinguished, they asked her to give in to him. There is a place on the east coast of the island where the land is torn apart, and it is said that, despite a struggle, Kamapua'a took her there (Kane, 1987). This story illustrates how men often defend other men who have raped or violated women. It calls to mind the Amber Heard case, in which the male media blasted her, and other men made a mockery of her case.

The curse of Pele is legendary. Many visitors to Kilauea have taken lava stones or black sand with them as souvenirs, only to find that their luck suddenly turned bad. People frequently return such souvenirs to The Hawaii Volcanoes National Park, reporting misfortune after taking them. One man reported that over the course of five years he had suffered 10 car accidents, two bad business ventures, and two cases of a broken heart. A woman wrote to the park detailing a streak of bad luck after she and her husband took a small vial of black sand: two hospitalizations and a job loss for him, as well as breakdowns of cars, televisions, and various appliances (Kane). Yet another woman detailed many mishaps that occurred after taking rocks, despite warnings at the site; she returned the stones and asked to be released from Pele's horrible spell. In the year 2000, park officials reported that over 2,000 pounds of rocks were returned annually.

These stories of misfortune may illustrate Pele's malevolent nature, but they may also be a lesson to tourists who desecrate the sacred nature of Pele's land by treating it merely as a source of souvenirs. Tourists taking stones or sand from Pele's land parallels the violation of Pele by Kamapua'a. In patriarchy, the land can be conquered and used, just like women's bodies.

There are several folk tales that give an indication of the character and disposition of Pele. In one of the stories, in her guise as an old woman, she approached two girls roasting breadfruit and asked for food. One of the girls shared her breadfruit, but the other refused, saying her food was devoted to another goddess. Shortly after, the house of the girl who declined was wiped out by molten lava, while the other girl's house was left intact. This story is one of many in which Pele takes revenge on those who will not share food, water, or cigarettes with her.

Another folk tale tells the story of a man who planted a banana tree and promised the first bunch to Pele. When it ripened, he did not see Pele, so he ate one of the bananas. Then Pele appeared and accused him of breaking his promise. He pleaded that they would have rotted otherwise and offered her a pick of any of the other bananas. She declined, with the retort that he promised them to her, whether or not they were rotten. She threatened to turn him to stone and then spewed her lava on him. He stands today as a humanoid lava stone on the volcanic landscape. The stories of Pele turning men to stone are similar to those about Medusa turning men to stone with her gaze. There is no evidence that the myths are connected historically, but both illustrate the superordinate power that wronged women have in reducing men to static, nonhuman forms.

There are countless stories of Pele as an old woman hitchhiker in a long white dress, sometimes barefoot but at other times without feet. She is usually seen hitching on lonely country roads on the Hawaiian Islands but has also been spotted as far away as Oregon, where she was observed near the eruption of Mount St. Helens in 1980. When picked up, she gets in the vehicle and asks for a cigarette, then mysteriously disappears, sometimes when the car is moving fast. A driver who picks her up does not receive any special favors, but those who pass her by usually encounter car trouble shortly thereafter. Her appearance as a hitchhiker usually signals an approaching eruption. Although she is a place-based goddess living in the crater of Kilauea, her magical capabilities enable her to travel wherever she likes, perhaps to test people's goodwill in giving her rides.

These stories illustrate that Pele is rageful, violent, vengeful, jealous, and capricious, seemingly motivated by her own self-interest. She is unlike many of the other dark goddesses, whose destructive tendencies are utilized to destroy an old social order in order to create a new one that is more just. Pele's powers seem more like the forces of nature, unbridled and unpredictable in an amoral sense. She does have both destructive and creative powers, but they are exercised on the land, not on the social fabric of a society. She sends out her lava flows over the land without regard to the humans who live there, unless, according to myth, she is seeking revenge on them. Her creative powers do, however, give rise to new and enlarged fertile landscapes from which fresh vegetation can grow—an ongoing, creative aspect of nature. Her sacred name is Pelehonuamea, which means "sacred person enlarging the earth" (Nimmo).

Rita Knipe, a Jungian analyst, gives a feminist interpretation of Pele. She describes Pele as "symbolic of the archetypal primeval emotions of anger, destruction and lust that lurk within us all, but especially within women who are constantly guarding to keep emotions under control that stem from their anger at repression in male dominated societies" (Nimmo). Pele is indeed an archetypal dark goddess whose repressed emotions mirror those of all women, especially those living under patriarchy. Many of those emotions may feel unacceptable to us, but only when we own them will we be free and fully aware of all parts of ourselves.

Pele has always been feared by Hawaiians, but she is also regarded with great affection and respect. She is called Madame Pele as well as Tutu (grandmother) Pele. Residents of the Big Island whose property has been destroyed by lava flows have an amazing equanimity about their losses, saying they understand that the land belongs to Pele, not to them. They also feel close to Pele because of their kinship with her as an ancestral relative from whom they are most likely directly descended. The people's close connection to Pele is also evident in the tradition of throwing parts of their relatives' bodies after death, including bones, fingernails, and locks of hair, into her caldera to live in the afterlife with the goddess, with whom they have a kinship tie.

Native Hawaiian traditions prescribe proper etiquette for those visiting Pele's home in the caldera, lest they encounter her wrath. Anyone who walks on her land must ask for her forgiveness. The ohelo berries, which grow on the first trees to spring up after a lava flow, are sacred to Pele; she requires people to make an offering of them before consumption. Pele is offended by menstruating women on her land, which is surprising given that she is a woman not given to patriarchal customs; however, women who are bleeding may safely visit her by carrying ti leaves for protection. Ti leaves also protect anyone who walks on her hot lava from burns on their feet. When visiting her home on the crater, offerings are considered necessary to appease her. They often consist of bottles of gin (which she apparently loves but are a substitute for awa, a native Hawaiian narcotic beverage), as well as red silk handkerchiefs and pigs (perhaps as revenge against the pig-god who raped her). There is no evidence that human sacrifices were ever made to Pele. Tourists who visit her leave a wide assortment of offerings, but the unfortunate result is that garbage, especially rotting food, must be removed from her home annually.

One of the best-known ceremonies in honor of Pele occurred in 1801, when Kamehameha I, who later united the Hawaiian Islands and became king, was worried that Pele's eruption would damage valuable land and fish ponds. He approached a kahuna (priest) and asked that he perform a ceremony to stop Pele's flow. The kahuna declined, saying that Kamehameha as chief must perform the required sacrifice himself. The chief was stricken with fear, but the kahuna assured him that he would not be killed. Kamehameha stood at the flow and threw in a lock of his hair. Pele accepted his sacrifice, and the flow stopped (Nimmo).

Pele's colors are red, orange, and black. She usually takes the form of a beautiful maiden with lighter brown skin than most Hawaiians (a racist trope common to many "dark" goddesses). She is also commonly seen as a feeble crone who walks with a cane. In both cases she is depicted wearing a white holoku—a long 19th-century dress with a train that is traditional Hawaiian formal wear (Nimmo). Mysteriously, many of the sightings claim that her feet are not visible, perhaps because as a spirit her feet don't touch the ground.

It is said that Pele, like many shape-shifting goddesses, takes over 400 human forms as well as many nonhuman forms such as fire, lighting, thunder, and earthquakes. Sometimes she is seen as a fireball that moves between Kilauea and Mauna Loa, presaging an eruption. At other times she takes the form of a white dog or is seen accompanied by a white dog. Sightings of the dog are relatively recent, the first noted in 1927, suggesting that her continued presence in the lives of Hawaiians is the inspiration for new myths. Other eyewitness reports date from the 1980s, citing the belief that when the white dog appears, an eruption is about to occur.

Pele is one of the few goddesses still revered in the world today. Many Hawaiians conduct ceremonies in her honor, even though the influx of missionaries in the early 19th century brought Christianity to the islands. Most Hawaiians converted to Christianity, but native beliefs were often preserved in personal and family ceremonies and became syncretic with Christian beliefs. The volcano area was far from any missionary outposts, so the native beliefs survived more easily there. Steen Bille, a Danish admiral who visited Pele in the mid-19th century, commented on the blend of old and new religious beliefs:

> The inhabitants have not by far abandoned their father's faith in Pele … even though they are baptized and in every way zealous Christians. … The great multitude believes at the same time that Pele still lives in the island. She is there as long as the volcano burns, they say, and the fact that Christ has not been able to expel her, they take as evidence of her powers. The faith in Pele will not disappear till Kilauea extinguishes her burning lake and the crater is covered by forests (Nimmo).

Pele made the news in the 1980s and '90s, when a geothermal energy project on Hawaii was proposed. Some Hawaiians interpreted Pele's eruptions as approval of the project, but others disagreed. In 1987, a group of Hawaiians took legal action against the drilling, saying it desecrated Pele's sacred land and violated their constitutional rights to worship her. They formed the Pele Defense Fund and presented their case to the Hawaii Supreme Court. Attorneys for the fund told the *Hawaii Advertiser* newspaper that Pele "is the heart of Hawaiian religious beliefs today; she daily inspires spiritual and physical life; geothermal development will diminish and finally extinguish her creative force, causing spiritual-religious, cultural, psychological and sociological injury and damage to the people who worship and live with Pele." One of the defenders of the Fund added: "We must protect her. … We can always develop energy, but we can never replace Pele" (Nimmo). The court ultimately decided that the project did not violate the constitutional rights of those wishing to worship Pele.

In response, in 1989 the Pele Defense Fund ran full-page ads in Hawaiian newspapers as well as the western edition of *The New York Times*, stating that drilling was "a brutal violation of native religious beliefs. … The volcano is a manifestation of Pele, the living Goddess sacred to Native Hawaiian religion. To violate Pele by drilling into her body is as outrageous to us as someone bulldozing the Sistine Chapel would be to Christians" (Nimmo). In 1988, the Fund appealed the case to the United States Supreme Court, which allowed the lower court ruling to stand.

The Pele Defense Fund then filed another motion to stop the geothermal project, claiming that it would not protect air quality standards. As the project progressed, approximately 350 Hawaiian gathered on the top of the mountain to build a traditional stone altar for Pele and perform chants and prayers for her. Even elderly people with difficulty walking made the trip out of devotion to her. One of the participants noticed a beautiful young woman with waist-length dark hair in a long, flowing white dress, calmly observing the scene. Then she disappeared into thin air, and it was assumed to be Pele showing approval of the altar. Despite the protest, the energy project workers took the altar apart, outraging the Hawaiians. One of the activists stated that building the altar was not meant as a protest but rather a ritual of healing for the violated Pele.

In 1990, protests by the Pele Defense Fund resumed, joined by The Big Island Rainforest Action Group, and 100 people were arrested. Noa Emmett Aluli, vice president of the Fund, went to

Washington, D.C., to lobby against a $15 million appropriation by Congress for the geothermal project. He remarked to a reporter, "Pele is the magma, Pele is the heat, Pele is the steam and especially the forests. … Geothermal will plunge into her very being. For us, this is sacrilege" (Nimmo). Interestingly, the Union of Indigenous Nations of Brazil joined the fight against destruction of the Hawaiian rainforest. The case against drilling on Pele is similar to many cases in which Native Americans have defended their sacred lands against drilling, pipelines, observatories, national monuments, and mining.

Eventually the drilling stopped because a well blew up, a rare occurrence which natives said was a sign of Pele's wrath. In 2006, Pele's land was transferred to the Hawaiian people under the Office of Hawaiian Affairs, a long-fought victory for the Fund and perhaps for Pele herself. And as a fierce goddess intimately connected to the land, Pele can serve as inspiration for the ecofeminist movement.

CHAPTER SEVENTEEN

Ecofeminism

"Ecofeminism is the idea that the oppression of women and the exploitation of the planet's natural resources are inextricably linked."
—Aiofe Coyne

The term "ecofeminism" was first coined by French feminist Francoise d'Eaubonne in 1974 in her book *Feminism or Death.* Ecofeminism looks at the parallels between the domination of women and the domination of nature; it also examines how the interests of feminism and the environment intersect. In patriarchy, women's bodies and the earth have been conflated, both seen as resources to be commodified and exploited. Thus, the oppression of women and the destruction of nature stem from the same root, capitalist and patriarchal society.

The Judaeo-Christian tradition has encouraged the alignment between women and nature. In Genesis, God gives Adam dominion over Eve, holding that she is rightfully subordinate to him but also proclaiming the "dominion mandate" that humans should dominate nature: "Be fruitful, and replenish the earth, and subdue it: and have dominion over the fish of the sea, and over the fowl of the air, and over every living thing that moveth upon the earth" (Bible, King James version). This passage can be interpreted to mean that humans are to be stewards of the earth, since they are instructed to replenish it, but what are the limitations on subduing the earth? The passage can be utilized to justify extracting resources from the earth, as with fracking, or leaving a large carbon footprint in order to create energy for human consumption. Genesis gives a hierarchical model of the world, with men on the top, women underneath them, and nature at the bottom (the dominator model). By contrast, feminism offers a more egalitarian model, supporting a partnership model between the sexes and harmony with nature. Ecofeminism, then, is an extension of this egalitarian view of the world.

Ecofeminism highlights how climate, the environment, and feminism are all interconnected and acknowledges how women can play a central role in defending and protecting the environment. Many feminist organizations around the world are dedicated to this mission: Women's Voices for the Earth (U.S.); Women's Environmental Network (Europe); and WoMin (Africa). These nonprofits have formed in large part because of their awareness that women are disproportionately impacted by climate change and environmental disasters. In her article "Climate change impacts women more than men," Mary Halton notes that 80% of people displaced by climate change are women (bbc, 2018). Because women have less economic power and are more likely to live in poverty, it is harder for them to adapt to weather crises. As primary caregivers and providers of food and fuel to their families, they are more vulnerable when floods or droughts occur. And in cases where families are headed by single women, they are more likely to be affected by environmental disasters that have a negative impact on jobs, infrastructure, and housing.

The environmental movement takes a stand against both patriarchy and capitalism because they are so intertwined. Capitalism, which sees everything as a resource, a commodity to be exploited, has played a huge role in the destruction of the environment for the purpose of creating wealth. The Amazon rainforests, for example, have been clear-cut for cattle farming, growing crops, mining, and timber cutting, all of which create economic benefit but have a devastating effect on the environment. An article in *Time* claims that the rainforest is near a tipping point which will be impossible to reverse. It explains that trees in the Amazon take up water, which is then released as rainfall, but with deforestation, the earth becomes dry scrubland, resulting in fires. "The battle for the Amazon is close to being lost," according to *Time*. "The emboldened forces of development are running without restraint, and the stakes for the planet couldn't be higher" (Sandy, 2019).

In the U.S., environmentalists have been fighting to prevent a similar despoliation of the environment. The protest at Standing Rock in North Dakota in 2016 was organized to block the Dakota Access Pipeline. It garnered media attention and brought environmental awareness to the country and the world. The "water protectors," as they were called, were defending the right to clean water on the Standing Rock Sioux reservation and the surrounding area. The pipeline's 1,200-mile route under the Missouri River threatened to pollute water from the river that provides drinking water to the 10,000 members of the tribe as well as millions of other people who live in the Missouri River Basin. As a result of the protest, the federal government decided to deny the permit to build the oil pipeline, but the following year it granted permission for the pipeline, which then spilled several times.

The Standing Rock protest was organized by the Sioux, or Lakota, tribe, but allies from all over the world joined the fight.[8] Women, in fact, were the backbone of the Standing Rock movement, according to Shannon Kring, a journalist who wrote about the protest for *Time* magazine (Kring, 2013).

"The women of Standing Rock are willing to risk their lives to stop the pipeline construction that desecrated their ancient burial and prayer sites and threatens their land, water, and very existence," she said. "They exemplify what it means to be an authentically empowered woman in the matrilineal way of being." She stressed that women have a special connection to "the land and waters, both of which are feminine in nature." Native women showed enormous fierceness and bravery, facing Mace, tear gas, rubber bullets, and attack dogs without relenting. Women stepping up to take leadership roles in the protest undoubtedly relates to the fact that Native women have typically had authority in decision-making processes for their tribes. "In interview after interview, the women in Standing Rock said that we are at the end of the patriarchal era of competition, aggression, and force," said Kring.

We may not be at the end yet, but the women of Standing Rock fought to bring about a change in the social paradigm to create a society in alignment with the Native American spiritual principle of protecting the environment for the next seven generations. In her interviews with Native women, Kring found a consensus that in the fight for environmental justice, women do not need to emulate men. They are standing their ground as

[8] Winona LaDuke, a Native American activist who is a member of the Ojibwe tribe, participated in the protest; she noted that "the leadership in a lot of the environmental movement and the indigenous movements has been women."

women, bearing out the idea that gender essentialism is false, as women can be just as ferocious and battle-worthy as men.

Lakota activist Rachelle Figueroa, who participated in the protest, said she was there to honor Mother Earth:

> She's everything. She's life. She brings life, she takes life. We get everything from her; we get our food, our shelter, medicines. ... That's why I came, mostly, was to pray, and to hold a sacred place so women would be able to come in and heal, and be able to have that strength–that rejuvenation that they need in order to keep doing what they're doing. It's going to be hard to get people back on track, but it's the women that will do it. It's the women that will stand up and say enough is enough (Zambelich & Alexandra, 2016).

LGBTQA+ people also had a key role in the protest. Zaria Howell, in an article in *THE 19th* (Zaria Howell, "Indigenous women and LGBTQ+ people led Dakota Access Pipeline protests," *THE 19th*, May 2021) wrote: "For many advocates, it was the first time they watched a movement that was led largely by women and queer folks around a unifying cause that was not based on gender" (Howell, 2021). Layha Spoonhunter, a member of the Eastern Shoshone and Northern Arapaho tribes who was part of the two-spirit[9] camp at the protest, remarked in the article that people from marginalized communities were at the forefront of the protest. "Standing Rock was a chance to go back to our own roots in terms of gender and sexuality," he said. "Being at Standing Rock and being around LGBT youth who, for maybe the first time, weren't afraid to express themselves and be in this community where you were actually welcomed,

[9] The term is used to describe Native Americans of a third gender which combines both male and female identities.

was a huge difference" (Howell). Here we see the intersection of environmentalism, feminism, and the LGBTQIA+ movement coming together for a common goal.

Older women are also a crucial component of the environmental movement. The Climate Grannies are a group of American women, both Native and non-Native, who have taken to activism as an expression of their values about preserving the environment. "They have the generational wisdom, environmental activism experience, free time—and they're not afraid of getting arrested" (Kutz, 2024). Jane Fonda, one of the best-known of the Climate Grannies, has been arrested several times for protesting and has her own PAC that supports climate activists running for office. Hazel Chandler, 78, a member of the Grannies, started her activism in 2016 with Elder Climate Action, a nonprofit that organizes older people to fight for environmental causes. More recently, she has been involved as an Arizona field coordinator of Moms Clean Air Force, a nonprofit that engages volunteers to work with lawmakers for climate justice. Older women from the Bay Area who participated in the Standing Rock protest formed their own organization, 1000 Grandmothers for Future Generations, upon their return to California. The group consists of older women, whether or not they are actually grandmothers, who have taken action on issues of divestment from the fossil fuel industry as well as legislative imperatives. Older women are in the vanguard of the climate justice movement, representing 61% of environmental activists today (Kutz).

Gaia

Gaia, a primordial Greek goddess, is the personification of the earth. Gaia was a Mother Goddess worshipped in Greece before the Hellenes introduced the cult of Zeus. As the daughter of Chaos, the original deity, her purpose was to create order out of

Gaia

Art and image © Lydia Ruyle.

chaos. She was the mother of the Giants as well as the Titans, one of whom is Cronus. She helped Cronus castrate his father, Uranus, her son and mate, because he was sexually abusing her. Uranus can be considered the first patriarch, as he was literally raping the earth, thus becoming the progenitor of a long line of men violating the earth. In typical patriarchal fashion, he was bested by his son Zeus, who became the most powerful god. When Zeus became ruler of the gods, Gaia was demoted and her power lessened.

Gaia, known as Mother Earth, was always seen as female, the ancestral mother. As a mother goddess, she is typically described as caring, nurturing, and life-sustaining—providing sustenance for all living creatures. In this regard she is a creative, life-giving deity, the source of all life. The Gaia hypothesis, first formulated by James Lovelock in the 1970s, holds that Gaia is a single, complex, self-regulating organism that creates the conditions for life on Earth (Boston, 2008). In this aspect Gaia is a benevolent earth goddess who created order out of chaos and became the precondition for life itself.

As a mother goddess, Gaia's nurturing, life-giving nature has been emphasized. However, like many other goddesses, she has a destructive, fierce side as well, which has been overlooked as part of her character. She can be an agent of massive destruction, with her tornadoes, hurricanes, thunderstorms, typhoons, cyclones, tropical storms, drought, floods, wildfires, heatwaves, heat domes, freezes and cold waves, and ice and hailstorms. Hurricane Katrina illustrated how powerful Gaia's destructive force can be; it caused nearly 1,500 fatalities and almost $200 billion in damage in the New Orleans area. As a result of climate change, hurricanes are more destructive and three times more frequent than 100 years ago (Environmental Defense Fund, 2024).

As climate change has worsened, extreme weather events have increased in frequency and intensity all around the world. Just as the myth of Gaia told the story of her helping Cronus castrate Uranus as revenge for abusing her, an enraged Gaia may be seeking retribution against humans for mistreating the earth with pollution, deforestation, fracking, burning fossil fuels, etc., as part of the capitalist exploitation of the environment which has caused global heating.

Scientists think that climate warming is also a factor in the increased incidence of epidemics from infectious diseases caused by floods that pollute drinking water and the migration/transmission of vector-borne pathogens into warmer areas. It may be that the disasters Gaia causes are her way of maintaining equilibrium in her self-regulating system so that the earth can survive despite the harm humans inflict on her. James Lovelock, originator of the Gaia hypothesis, states that the COVID epidemic may have been Earth's way of trying to protect herself. If we don't take the climate crisis seriously, he speculates, "Gaia will try harder next time with something even nastier" (Lovelock, 2021).

Gaia may in fact be working in her own way to create climate justice. If this is the case, Gaia resembles many of the fierce goddesses who destroy old systems to create ones that are more just. As the personification of the earth itself, she shows herself to be both a fructifying, life-giving goddess as well as a fierce, destructive goddess whose "actions" and patterns are designed to bring about a more just environment.

Witches Embody Fierce Goddess Energy

As a primordial goddess, Gaia is deeply connected to the wilderness and natural remedies that the earth produces. Historically, witches were lay healers who were in close touch with the earth, using herbal remedies to heal the sick and aid in the labor and delivery process. They had an intimate knowledge of women's reproductive capacity and used herbs for contraception and abortion.

With the powers witches had over reproduction, they threatened the new male medical establishment during the European Renaissance. The rise of this new profession, under the auspices of the ruling classes, led to the persecution of witches on "medical" grounds during "the Burning Times" (roughly the 15th to 18th centuries). The ruling classes also used the witch trials as a means of appropriating land owned by witches for themselves, many of whom were single women with little power; widows comprised approximately 10%-20% of the population at the time (UAB, 2022). The suppression of witches was an early historical occurrence of men suppressing women as healers.

Hecate, queen of the witches, was the great granddaughter of Gaia, placing her in the tradition of fierce goddesses with power over all nature. Contemporary witches, many of whom worship Hecate today, are real-life representatives of fierce goddess energy and power. Starhawk, an avowed witch living today, is a global justice activist and founder of the Reclaiming Collective, a group that blends pagan spirituality with environmental activism. Starhawk says her passion is "to integrate more closely the worship of nature with knowledge that comes from the observation of nature, and to infuse science, ecological design, and environmental activism with the deep connectedness that comes from acknowledging the sacred" (Starhawk, 1999). She has been one of the leaders of the international permaculture movement, which creates ecosystems that are sustainable and self-sufficient. Her environmental activism, which addresses ecosystem degradation on a massive scale, is designed to counteract the effects of climate change.

Social justice and ecofeminism are intimately intertwined, and restoring the planet to ecological health will require that the rights of marginalized people be addressed. The sidelining of BIPOC and other marginalized people has hampered both traditional feminism and environmentalism. Leah Thomas, in her book *The Intersectional Environmentalist: How to Dismantle Systems of Oppression to Protect People + Planet*, states: "We cannot save the planet without uplifting the voices of those most marginalized" (Thomas, 2022). She points out that the underrepresentation of various marginalized groups (BIPOC, Asian, LGBTQ+, disabled, and low socioeconomic status) has stifled environmentalism because the liberation of all people and the planet requires that the interconnection between the two be taken into account. Historically, environmental movements in the Global North have not been as inclusive as those in the Global South; the former have not given adequate representation to marginalized peoples, and in particular to communities of color, which have fewer environmental protections in place. "People of color in the U.S. and around the world are bearing the brunt of the climate crisis and environmental injustice," says Thomas. The earth will not be healed until the intersectional nature of the planet and its peoples is understood and addressed.

We need to honor and respect Gaia as a fierce goddess working in her own way to preserve the environment, using creative as well as destructive means. Gaia reminds us that we must take care of her, regarding her as sacred rather than a resource to be plundered, pillaged, and exploited. Ecofeminist policies that support the rights of women and other marginalized people, as well as the well-being of the earth, must be pursued hand in hand. Only then will we be able to ensure a sustainable future for seven generations of people living harmoniously with Mother Earth.

CHAPTER EIGHTEEN

Feminism, the LGBTQ+ Movement, and Fierce Goddesses

This is where feminist and LGBTI movements meet:
the ill-treatment of women in our societies and the
ill-treatment of LGBTI persons have the same root cause.
— Julia Ehrt

Feminism intersects with the LGBTQ+ movement because patriarchy also oppresses LGBTQ+ people, who do not conform to the roles and expectations for men and women under a patriarchal paradigm. These two movements can work together to move beyond patriarchy.

There have been deities who reflect gay and lesbian orientations, showing that humans have not historically been exclusively heterosexual. There are many gods who engage in sex with other men. Greek mythology has a panoply of male gods who relate to other male gods, such as Apollo and Adonis, as well as male gods who have sex with mortals, e.g., Zeus and Aetos. Sexual relationships between men were common in Greek culture, which may explain such same-sex liaisons between deities, whose actions often mimic those of humans.

However, there is a paucity of lesbian goddesses, perhaps because so many cultures, especially those that are patriarchal, were androcentric. Some of the devotees of Erzulie Danto, a goddess of African origin (see below) regard her as lesbian, although the myths surrounding her do not emphasize a same-sex orientation. The Inuit goddess Sedna is sometimes described as lesbian, but myths about her differ in this regard; one story says that she lives at the bottom of the ocean with her female partner, Qailertetang, goddess of hunters, whereas another story portrays her as married to a man who betrays her (perhaps she was better off as a lesbian). Some scholars postulate that Diana (Artemis in the Greek pantheon) was lesbian, but myths actually describe her as an independent, chaste goddess who does not welcome sex with anyone, perhaps representing asexual people.

Lesbians today face challenges that their heterosexual counterparts do not. Their right to same-sex marriage has been called into question by the Supreme Court. And wage inequality for women means that lesbian couples have a lower combined income than hetero or gay male couples. They face discrimination in employment and housing. Social stress related to stigma and prejudice also puts lesbians at higher risk of mental disorders and distress. The way in which lesbians have been marginalized in the feminist movement resonates with the way BIPOC women have also been marginalized.

Lesbian feminism analyzes and condemns the institution of marriage as oppressive, as it grew out of the historical condition of women as the property, or chattel, of men. It is not based on women's sexual desire for each other, although that may exist; rather, it champions a political movement aimed at empowering women by freeing them from male supremacy and domination by men. Growing out of the second wave of the women's liberation movement, it has operated as a resistance to man-made institutions.

Like BIPOC women, lesbians have historically found themselves marginalized within the feminist movement. In 1970, Betty Friedan commented that lesbians represented a “lavender menace” to the women’s movement (Napisopi, 2019). Friedan was concerned that a focus on lesbians would derail the new wave of the movement and inhibit passage of the ERA. Her remark angered lesbians, who organized their own group called the Radicalesbians; they pronounced that “a lesbian is the rage of all women condensed to the point of explosion” (Saraswati, 2021). In response to Friedan, they distributed their manifesto, “The Woman-Identified Woman,” at the Second Congress to Unite Women in 1970, a conference sponsored by NOW (National Organization of Women). Friedan expelled lesbians from the New York chapter of NOW in 1970 but was replaced as the president of NOW shortly thereafter. The next year, NOW declared that “a woman’s right to her own person includes the right to define and express her own sexuality” (Griffith).

After not being supported by heterosexual feminists, radical lesbians began to espouse separatism from men as a way of consolidating female power and disengaging from male-dominated institutions. Their strategy was to help women focus their time and energy on each other, apart from men. Some lesbians even bought land so they could live together. In 1973, a group of Black lesbians called the Combahee River Collective formed in Boston to address the intersecting oppressions of race, class, gender, and sexual orientation. They drew attention to racism and the gender-only approach within the white feminist movement and were the first to use the term “identity politics.” They disbanded in 1980 but left a legacy of increased emphasis on the importance of an intersectional approach to the liberation of all women.

It is imperative that feminists cleave together, lesbian and straight, in an intersectional movement that unites women in a true sisterhood. Only then will we be unified and strong enough to move the feminist agenda forward.

In recent years, transgender, nonbinary, and gender-fluid people have become a more visible part of the LGBTQ+ movement. These gender identities differ from a cisgender identity, in which a person's gender identity matches their biological sex. The umbrella term "queer" applies to gender-variant folks as well as to people who engage in same-sex sexual relations. People with nonconforming gender identities also face discrimination and oppression under patriarchy. These identities are not seen as valid in a system based on strict, binary gender roles. Transgender women face the same institutional inequalities that cisgender women do, along with marginalization because of their transgender identity, even within the feminist movement. Meanwhile, transgender men who are female-bodied face similar obstacles as cisgender women when it comes to reproductive rights and bodily autonomy. Therefore, the concerns and goals of people with nonconforming gender identities intersect with those of feminism. Since ancient times, nonconforming gender identities have also been acknowledged and enshrined in myths, reflecting the lived reality that people don't always fall into rigid categories determined by biological sex. The existence of transgender, nonbinary, and gender-fluid people and deities strengthens the argument against gender essentialism (as discussed in chapter 13). Several African and Afro-Caribbean goddesses represent deities that do not fall into discrete categories of the gender binary.

Mami Wata

One of the most ancient goddesses, Mami Wata has been venerated for thousands of years, primarily in west, central, and southern Africa, as well as recently in the African diaspora. She is one of the most powerful goddesses in the Voodoo religion, both loved and feared. She is a mermaid whose waters can be used for healing or destruction. Mami Wata embodies opposites, including sickness and health, danger and safety, land and sea. Some devotees in Nigeria enter into a spiritual marriage with her in which they are "married in the water." Mami Wata herself is gender-fluid, transforming at times into both male and female deities; as such, she identifies with and marries people of different genders. Thus, she is a goddess who can provide inspiration for people who are gender-fluid and queer.

Mami Wata is depicted with a large snake coiled around her and in some Christianized countries has become associated with Santa Marta, who is pictured with a snake or dragon. As a beautiful mermaid, she combs her long hair and beholds herself in a golden mirror. Her devotees wear her colors—white for spirituality and red for blood and violence. She is believed to haunt shores, capturing swimmers and sailors. If she favors one of them, she will return them to shore unharmed and transformed spiritually as well as materially (often with great wealth). If she finds them unworthy, they might see the bottom of the sea instead. Even today people in Cameroon hold her wrath responsible for any deaths that occur when swimmers are swept out to sea with undertows. Celebrations of Mami Wata include music and dance, and sometimes she takes possession of the dancers in trance (RealMermaids, 2024).

The image of Mami Wata as a double-tailed mermaid is recognizable in the logo of Starbucks, although the company claims it found the image in a book about Norse mythology. The

Mami Wata

Art by Erika Busse.

German perfume company Dralle has used the image of Mami Wata as a mermaid gazing into a mirror on its perfume bottles. This goddess has eternal, as well as commercial, appeal, or perhaps eternal commercial appeal (Dorsey, 2020). Mami Wata has made it into the contemporary international music scene with traditional chants and rap by artists such as N'Deye, Skip & Die, and Sa-Roc—a testament to her lasting appeal.

Mawu-Lisa

The Fon, a warlike people of Dahomey, West Africa (now the Republic of Benin), consider the deity Mawu-Lisa to be the creator of the world, taking over creation from the deity Nana Buruku and imposing order on the universe. While Mawu-Lisa created the earth, a cosmic serpent carried the deity around in his mouth. The serpent's undulations shaped the landscape, and its excrement created the mountains. After Mawu-Lisa finished creating, the snake wrapped itself around the earth to hold it in place. When the snake moved, it caused earthquakes, and when it revolved around the earth, it caused the sky to move.

On the first day after finishing creation, Mawu-Lisa gave birth to seven children, who became the central deities of the Fon pantheon. On the second day, Mawu-Lisa made Earth habitable and on the third day gave humans sight and speech. On the last day, Mawu-Lisa gave humans the skills necessary to survive. Finally, Mawu-Lisa divided the realms of the universe among the seven children—the earth, thunder and lightning, the seas, the hunt, the air, and iron. The last child was left with no realm to preside over, so he became Mawu-Lisa's messenger, able to travel among all the realms.

After creating the world, Mawu-Lisa asked Awe, the monkey created afterward, to help out by making some animals out of clay. He did so but tried unsuccessfully to breathe life

Mawu-Lisa

Art by Erika Busse.

into them, blowing on them but only causing them to move with the force of his breath rather than bursting into life. Mawu-Lisa, angry at Awe's arrogance, reminded him that he did not possess the power of creation and fed him porridge with the seed of death in it.

Mawu-Lisa is actually a synthesis of two gods, Mawu and Lisa, who united into one deity, creating balance between opposing forces of the universe. Mawu is the female aspect, ruling over the moon and night while embodying nurturance, motherhood, and fertility. Lisa represents the male aspect, which presides over the sun and daytime, a fierce warrior god manifesting strength, courage, and virility. Like many of the dark goddesses, this twin deity expresses both the creative and destructive aspects of divinity. As a two-in-one force, Mawu-Lisa, sometimes referred to simply as Mawu, is not just a deity but actually the Supreme Being, highest on the list of divinities. Mawu-Lisa is an unusual nonbinary deity who transcends male and female binaries. They (plural pronoun used for nonbinary individuals) are one of the few divinities that queer and gender nonconforming people can identify with and worship.

Mawu-Lisa can also be an inspiration for all women who have suffered under colonialism. Mawu-Lisa motivated Dahomean women to be keepers of their culture. The transatlantic slave trade disrupted Dahomean religious life, but women used Voodoo rituals honoring Mawu-Lisa to combat colonial structures. In "African Traditional Religions: Mawu's Legacy and Women's Power in Haitian Vodou and the Diaspora," Malisha Frawley states, "Pre-colonial evidence illustrates that Dahomean women were fierce protectors of the royal cult and … women continue to be regarded as the custodians of Dahomean culture in the post-colonial era by using evidence from the Haitian revolution and the ability of Haitian Mambos (priestesses) to intensify the symbol of Mawu-Lisa in the diaspora" (Frawley, 2023).

Thus, women who venerated Mawu-Lisa helped keep that deity alive and ensure the resistance of Voodoo to the colonial system of oppression. The Mambos may have experienced inequalities in various parts of their lives in the diaspora, but during rituals, when they invoked Haitian spirits to improve the well-being of the community, they were not limited by social or political constraints. In such rituals, Mambos achieved a spiritual power grounded in community experience rather than theological scriptures with prescribed hierarchical leadership roles. The lack of hierarchy appealed to a feminine worldview and primarily encouraged the participation of women.

Erzulie Danto

Erzulie Danto, a dark-skinned deity of African origin, became part of Haitian Vodou and New Orleans Voodoo after slaves were brought to the New World. She is a protector of women and children, especially those who are abused by men.

Like many dark goddesses, Erzulie Danto is known for both her nurturing and fierce aspects. She is a devoted mother figure who takes care of children but is also a strict disciplinarian, intolerant of bad behavior. Dedicated to children, she will do anything for them, finding solutions for all their problems. She loves dolls and often receives dolls as gifts. She is sometimes pictured as the Virgin Mary because of the influence of Christianity on Vodou. Before slaves were freed, they were not allowed to practice their indigenous religion, so they incorporated elements of Christianity, praying to Catholic saints and creating icons for worship that disguised their religious practices. As a result, Erzulie Danto became a syncretized form of the Black Madonna, often identified with Our Lady of Czestochowa in Poland.

Erzulie Danto

Art and image © Lydia Ruyle.

She is a symbol of resistance and empowerment of all women, as well as a patron of LGBTQ+ individuals. Some of her followers regard her as a lesbian. In 2019, a rainbow halo, symbolic of the Pride movement, was added to her depiction as the Black Madonna of Czestochowa, generating blowback from the Catholic Church. Those accused of mounting posters with the rainbow halo were arrested for religious heresy. Amnesty International gave support to the hundreds of protestors in Warsaw carrying images known as the 10,000 Rainbow Marys. Eventually all those arrested were acquitted. The rainbow halo icon has grown beyond Polish borders, occupying a prominent role in the GayChurchBerlin; it was even utilized in a worship service in an interfaith community in Enid, Oklahoma, in 2021 (Cherry, 2024).

Erzulie Danto is always pictured with one of her two children—her son, Ti Jean Petwo, or her daughter, Anais, who serves as her translator or interpreter because Erzulie Danto is mute and deaf; her tongue was cut out by her own followers, who feared that she would give away their secrets if captured in battle.

Known as a "hot" spirit, Erzulie Danto also has an aggressive, unruly side. In battle, she is so strong that she can endure seven stabbings, vomiting blood into a basin and giving it to her enemy as a form of spite. The dances to honor her are nearly violent, and sometimes those who experience possession by her in a trance state vomit blood. She is sometimes confused with Ezili Red Eyes, a related spirit who may actually be Erzulie Danto when she is angry. Trance possession by this spirit can result in the devotee's eyes turning red very quickly.

Erzulie Danto has a long-standing antagonism with her sister Erzulie Freda. The two of them fought over a man, and during the fight, Erzulie Danto stabbed her sister in the heart, whereupon Erzulie Freda removed the knife and cut her sister on the face. The scars from the cut are pictured in icons of Erzulie Danto, which are suggestive of scarification rituals in African religions. Marinette, who is discussed in an earlier chapter, was a priestess of Erzulie Danto; Marinette became possessed by her during a ceremony in which a pig was sacrificed and a pact written in the pig's blood, which culminated in a slave revolt against the French and the eventual formation of the Republic of Haiti.

Erzulie Danto's colors are navy blue and blood red. She often dresses in blue denim, which devotees wear to honor her. She loves Florida water (a cologne of lemon, bergamot, and cinnamon), which she sometimes drinks, and is fond of Reve D'Or perfume. She smokes strong, unfiltered cigarettes and sometimes cigars. She likes double-edged daggers and silver jewelry with blue or red stones. She receives offerings of alcoholic beverages which she enjoys, including red wine, beer, and creme de cacao. A smart businesswoman, she sells pigs in the market to support her children, and she brings luck in business matters to those who honor her. Her symbol, or sigil, is a heart-shaped veve—a diagram of a cross-hatched heart that has magical significance in bringing about an outcome the user intends.

Erzulie Danto is popular today in Haiti and is still honored by musical artists, including New York City jazz artist Cecil Taylor, whose 1989 album is titled "Erzulie Maketh Saint," and singers Monvelyno and Riva Precil, who perform a song called "Erzulie."

These fierce goddesses challenge traditional, Western, patriarchal ideas about gender and sexuality as well as racism and colonial oppression. They represent the power that feminists can draw both from the fierce goddesses and from each other in a truly intersectional movement.

Persephone
Shutterstock standard image licensed.

Conclusion

"[Persephone] guides us through the shadowy realms
of our subconscious to face our demons and fears so that
we might rise again in the light of our personal power and
potential and claim that which we desire."
— Robin Corak

One of the most famous myths of all time centers around the Greek goddess Persephone's abduction (sometimes understood as a rape) by Hades, god of the underworld. Persephone was the daughter of Demeter, goddess of agriculture, and Zeus, king of the gods. In her maiden aspect she was known as Kore, which was not a name but rather a term meaning "girl."

One beautiful spring day Kore was enjoying the flowering hillsides when her attention was caught by a most appealing flower, a narcissus. As she reached down to pick it, the ground near her opened up, and Hades emerged with his chariot. She was filled with fear, but Hades grabbed her and descended to his realm below the earth. Demeter, unable to find her daughter, became depressed and neglected her duties of taking care of the earth. She searched tirelessly for Persephone, who was nowhere to be found. As Demeter's depression deepened, winter overtook the earth; plants died, and the earth became barren. Persephone missed her mother and longed to return to her. But she was torn because Hades professed his love for her and explained that Zeus had engineered her abduction.

Meanwhile, Demeter continued to wander the earth and, in a state of exhaustion, decided to rest in Eleusis. Four young women found her and, not recognizing her, invited her to stay for a while in their home. Their parents entrusted her to take care of their young son. As a favor to them, Demeter tried to give the son immortal life by immersing him in fire each night and removing him before dawn. The mother found him in flames one night and, shocked at her discovery, asked Demeter to leave. At that point Demeter revealed her identity, and the family asked for her forgiveness. Demeter demanded that they build her a temple where her secret to immortality would be taught. The family agreed and asked the town to build the temple, which Demeter blessed before moving on to continue her search for her daughter.

(This part of the story, in which Demeter uses fire to give immortal life to the child she was taking care of, is an obvious reference to the myth of Isis, who is known as Demeter in Greek, according to Herodotus. Isis's assimilation into Demeter typifies the way so many fierce goddesses have survived and morphed into others, entering different cultures as time goes on; such goddesses have even survived inside patriarchal cultures, indicating the universal, enduring aspect of them as archetypes.)

Demeter, filled with rage after discovering Zeus's plot to have Persephone abducted, traveled to Mount Olympus and demanded that Zeus return her. To appease Demeter, Zeus dispatched Hermes to the underworld to bring her back; Hecate accompanied him, as a fierce goddess was needed to transcend life and death. Hermes was surprised to find that Persephone was no longer an immature maiden; instead, she had become a regal Queen of the Dead who greeted new arrivals and helped them adjust to her domain. And even though Persephone missed her mother, she did not want to leave her husband. Feeling torn between them, Persephone decided to eat pomegranate seeds, knowing that if she ate anything in the underworld, she would belong to it and have to remain there. (In an alternate version, Hades forces the seeds into her mouth.) However, she only ate six seeds, knowing that meant she would spend six months with Hades and six months above ground with her mother.

With Hecate, Hermes brought Persephone back from the Underworld. Demeter, overjoyed at her daughter's return, made the earth green again. She noticed, however, that her daughter had changed into a powerful goddess and wondered if they would ever be the same again.

Persephone was happy that she could spend half the year on the earth with her mother and half the year with her husband. Each year when she descended to Hades, her mother's mourning would cause winter to come; but when she ascended, her mother's joy would wake up the earth in spring. Persephone's coming and going from the Underworld was thus responsible for changes in the seasons ever after. As a goddess of grains and vegetation, Persephone, like her mother, is tied to nature, representing the tie between women and nature discussed in the ecofeminism chapter.

Persephone's journey to the Underworld symbolizes her transition from an immature young girl to a wise woman. She started out as a naive maiden, picking flowers on the hillside, and transformed into a sovereign queen. Before she descended, she lacked her own identity; she needed to explore her interior world before she could become her full, individuated self. Persephone picking a narcissus flower triggered her descent; when she plucked it, the earth opened up in the hole it left, and Hades emerged to abduct her. The narcissus represents her narcissistic concern with her own youth and beauty, which had to be shed for her to become a mature woman concerned with the fate of her subjects in the Underworld. When Persephone returns to the light of day, she is wiser than before, reuniting with her mother as an equal. Persephone's transformation from young maiden to wise woman is reminiscent of Vasilisa's journey, activated by Baba Yaga, of coming into full power and wholeness by embracing her shadow.

Persephone's journey to the Underworld and back represents the eternal cycle of life, death, and rebirth. That cycle formed the basis of rites known as the Eleusinian Mysteries in Greece. The rites took place in Eleusis, the place where Demeter asked that a temple be built for her. Since those who participated in the rites were sworn to secrecy, we don't know the details, but they centered on the symbolism of the agricultural cycle. The myth of Demeter and Persephone was central to how the rites were enacted, leading participants through the process of death and rebirth. Rites involved drinking a special mix of herbs and barley with an added hallucinogen derived from the fungus ergot. The sacred drink may have helped in experiencing the transformation from death to life and relinquishing any fears related to it. "Rites honoring Persephone … included processions in the fall that involved pausing at numerous shrines that reflected the powers of generation of both Demeter and Kore and those of the death god, Hades," says Courtney Weber in *Hekate: Goddess of Witches*. "This suggests that Demeter's mysteries were deeper than the soil, connecting her with human mortality and the afterlife" (Weber, 2021). Similarly, many fierce goddesses, including Isis and Kali, preside over the mysteries of life, death, and rebirth, which may more broadly symbolize women's power to create life or decide whether or not to bring new life into the world.

Another myth that speaks to Persephone's power concerns the wild bull named Cerus, whom people feared because he created mayhem and destruction by trampling their villages. After returning to the upper world, Persephone tamed him, turning him into a docile creature she could ride. When she returned to the Underworld, Cerus turned into the constellation Taurus.

This story shows the transformative power of Persephone's stay in the Underworld. She returns with a greater wisdom that has a civilizing effect on the world, especially the unbridled, destructive aspects of masculinity represented by the bull. When she was a maiden picking flowers, an encounter with the bull might have been deadly to her. After all, the bull represents Zeus, who raped and abducted Europa as a white bull. But after her time in the Underworld, confronting her own inner darkness, Persephone discovered a source of female power that created balance between the masculine and the feminine—like other fierce goddesses who incorporate that balance, thus contradicting gender essentialism and blurring the gender binary. After Persephone's empowerment from her descent into darkness, she became a ruler of her own domain, the Underworld, on a par with Zeus as ruler over Mount Olympus.

When women lean into their own inner strength by integrating the dark aspects of their psyches, they are no longer subject to being overpowered by men. The masculine aspects of the universe, no longer violent and threatening, are themselves transformed into a beautiful constellation of stars that shines brightly while Persephone is in the Underworld. Her darkness in the Underworld and Zeus's lights in Taurus create a harmony in the universe, a union of opposites. When Persephone ascends to the upper world, the bull descends from the heavens to her; she rides him in perfect harmony, bringing joy and bounty to the universe.

The approximately 20 fierce goddesses highlighted in this book give credence to the idea that there are no essential differences in temperament between women and men. These goddess figures, as female archetypes, represent those aspects of women that often live in the shadows of the psyche. But when women claim the dark parts of themselves, they have the capacity to experience rage and destructive impulses just as much as men.

With so many goddesses from different cultures and time periods displaying a pugnacious nature, it becomes hard to deny that women can be just as fierce as men. And when women do show their fierceness, it isn't because they are imitating men or becoming like them. They are expressing their deep and unsettled relationship to injustices they have experienced firsthand as women. They come by anger and rage naturally as a result of living in unjust societies that treat them as second-class citizens; the violence they have suffered at the hands of men is by itself sufficient cause of rage. The fierce goddesses provide strong examples for women in owning their rage and fighting the injustices that deprive them of their rights. These goddesses, as archetypes, have carried female rage over the millennia.

The story of Hathor and Sekhmet is a great illustration of how a loving and peaceful goddess, Hathor, can, when confronted with injustice, become mobilized with anger and transformed into a figure (Sekhmet) who fights to eradicate the wrong. Sekhmet came into existence when Hathor realized the rage that brewed within her.

The dark goddesses, as well as the Gulaab Gang and Iranian women today, are motivated to fight injustice with anger and rage. When rage is put to use in countering injustice, it becomes sacred rage. It's not surprising that anger and rage are seen as unacceptable for women, as these emotions lead them to take action against injustice. Patriarchal systems that wish to preserve the status quo must oppress women by conditioning them to be meek and pliable; in that way they keep women in their place, not questioning the patriarchal worldview. Women who seem to be complacent and accommodating members of society have the potential to become virulent activists when they connect to their own inner rage about the injustices they have suffered.

Rage is the fuel that drives social change. Even though rage is often considered a negative emotion, it is actually a hopeful emotion that looks to the future for needed change. It creates the possibility of change rather than a passive acceptance of things as they are. Rage that is elicited by social inequality becomes a driving force for fair and egalitarian political systems. Rage is transformative, leading to the destruction of oppressive systems in favor of equal opportunities for advancement and participation in society by all people.

The fierce goddesses carry the energy of destruction of unjust social orders as well as the energy to create new, more just ones. In touch with the death and rebirth process, they help us destroy the old to make room for the new. Alive in our collective unconscious, they are speaking to us across the centuries. If we listen, they can infuse us with the energy to fight for our rights and transform patriarchy into a more egalitarian, female-honoring social system. These goddesses are sending a timeless message to us as feminists today, urging us to reclaim the anger and rage that live in the shadow of our psyches in order to dismantle patriarchy.

When women own the anger and rage that live in their shadows, they individuate, becoming whole people who have access to all parts of themselves. Spiritual bypass, rooted in the belief that everything in the world is progressing as it should, causes people to deny their negative feelings as well as the very real and pressing problems in society. It truncates people's emotional development into full and balanced human beings, in touch with both their light and dark sides. The fierce goddesses model for women how to achieve wholeness through integrating the dark aspects of their psyches.

The dark, or fierce, goddesses, help us address the problem of intersectionality, which has plagued feminism since its inception. White women have been at the forefront of the feminist movement, shunting Black and Brown women into the sidelines. For feminism to achieve its goal of liberating women, it must create a coalition of women of different races and ethnicities. Only then can women unite as a powerful front, with both race and gender contributing to an intersectional analysis.

The dark goddesses show us a way forward in creating an intersectional movement. Since virtually all of them are dark-skinned, they stand for those women who have often been left behind by the movement. They are archetypal women of color who represent not just women but also racial minorities that have been the most disenfranchised. The dark goddesses are truly revolutionary in marshaling their power in ways that don't depend on white privilege. They may have even more reason to be enraged because of ways they have been shortchanged by society. When these dark goddesses, with their dark skin, are integrated into our psyches, they can then symbolically lead an intersectional movement for all women. The rage they carry at being on the margins of society, suffering oppression as a result of both race and gender, positions them to be the tip of the spear in the fight to eradicate patriarchy.

The fierce goddesses have carried women's wisdom through the ages, preserved in myths and fairy tales. And even when they were coopted by patriarchal religions, they survived in their respective guises. These stories have endured because they help women evolve into full, vital human beings who are in touch with their own truth.

Feminism needs a fresh infusion of energy from the fierce goddesses to continue to fight for women's rights, such as reproductive rights, equal pay, and inalienable rights such as the right to satisfactory and comprehensive health care. These goddesses are sending a message for us today that transcends time, if we are willing to listen. They are inviting us to tap into their fierce energy, which can rejuvenate the flagging women's movement. Their energy, which the movement desperately needs, is the fuel for our fight. We need to honor and listen to the wisdom that the fierce goddesses can impart to us today. Doing so will help infuse the stagnancy of the feminist movement with the fierce energy needed to rise up, with renewed vigor, in fighting for our rights and throwing off the yoke of patriarchy.

Afterword

The election of Donald Trump as the 47th President of the United States on November 5, 2024, was a shock to those of us who expected Kamala Harris to win. The polls had shown a toss-up between the two candidates, which turned out to be inaccurate. Just as I had done when Hillary Clinton ran against Trump in 2016, I stayed up until knew the outcome of the race. Grief overcame me as the reality of a Trump win seeped in. I burst into tears, as I had done with Clinton's loss, but the grief was far worse this time.

So much was at stake, from climate change to reproductive rights to the rights of women generally. It seemed unbelievable to me that the worst man in America—an admitted sexual predator, a convicted rapist, a felon, a racist, a xenophobe, a liar, an insurrectionist—could win against a qualified, experienced woman who, unlike Clinton, was considered by many to actually be likable. The fact that Harris is a woman of color created a double loss for her supporters—not only the loss of a first female president but also the loss of a female, BIPOC president.

Trump's win was a crushing blow to my hopes and dreams for a better, more just society. I strongly believed before the election that as a country we were not going back but instead going forward. The election outcome was another huge wake-up call for me, alerting me to the reality that women's reproductive rights would be eroded even more than they were when Roe was overturned. Looking ahead to women's rights being stripped even further, I felt a heavy weight pulling me downward into the depths of despair.

After a few days of tending my despair, I came to the realization that despair is a luxury that we as women cannot afford to indulge in right now. As an equestrian, I know that when one falls off a horse, it's imperative to get right back on. We need to get back on the project of fighting for women's rights, with even more determination than before. If we don't mount a timely counterattack on Trump's draconian policies toward women, we stand to lose even more ground. Already women are dying from lack of reproductive care or facing criminal charges for "child endangerment." My despair morphed into rage as I realized the atrocities awaiting women, especially if a national abortion ban (which Trump would not rule out) is enacted.

Many young women in the U.S. are also experiencing anger and rage. Young American women are understandably angry at men who voted for Trump, who in his previous term added three conservative justices to the Supreme Court to overturn Roe. Since the election, social media are replete with examples of American women forgoing men, modeled on the feminist 4B movement in South Korea in the mid- to late 2010s.

Such women are determined not to engage romantically with men, abiding by the tenets of 4B, all of which start with "bi" in Korean, meaning "no": no sex with men, no dating, no marriage, no childbirth. South Korean women are hoping that 4B will undermine the structure of patriarchy, which has exerted a strong hold on the Korean culture, as evidenced by traditional beauty standards, revenge porn, femicide, spycams, and sexual assaults. South Korea also suffers from an unequal political climate (women hold just 17% of parliament seats) as well as inequalities in wages and earned income.

It's too early to know whether the 4B will catch on and have an impact in the U.S. But in the wake of the election, women are posting on Instagram and TikTok about the advantages of a 4B life. "We have pandered and begged for men's safety and done all the things that we were supposed to, and they still hate us," Ashli Pollard, a 36-year-old from St. Louis, told CNN. "So if you're going to hate us, then we're going to do what we want" (Kaur, 2024). Pollard has sworn off men since 2022 and reports that a life that decenters men has helped her be more in touch with herself and has led to her feeling better off on her own. Women who are decentering men in their lives have embraced a "boysober" lifestyle that forgoes romantic relationships in favor of platonic ones.[10]

According to a recent article in *The New York Times*, the past year, even before Trump's win, has seen an "explosion" of women who say they are deleting dating apps, as well as women celebrities who have opted for a celibate life or who consider themselves "self-partnered." And older millennial and Gen X women disillusioned with marriage have taken to writing divorce memoirs. Online, women are promoting sexual independence with the use of vibrators and turning to self-defense with guns, rejecting protection by men. The *sine qua non* for many women after a Trump victory is outrage at the patriarchal system that marginalizes and oppresses women. Rage becomes the fuel that drives women into forgoing men as a way of undermining misogynistic culture.

Disillusionment with heterosexual relationships has led to "heteropessimism," a term coined by gender scholar Asa Seresin, who defined it in 2019 as "performative disaffiliations

---

[10] The term "boysober" was originated by comedian Hope Woodward, who embarked on a break from heterosexual dating and sex.

with heterosexuality, usually expressed in the form of regret, embarrassment, or hopelessness about straight experience" (Seresin, 2019). Clearly, the seeds of heteropessimism were sown years before Trump was reelected, but they have grown into a social movement that is taking off in response to the resurgence of domination of women by men and the backlash against women's rights, especially reproductive rights.

If women forgo romantic relationships with men, will they be drawn to lesbianism? Many radical feminists have espoused lesbian relationships as a political statement against patriarchy. Radical lesbianism, which arose during the second wave of the women's movement, opposes heterosexual relationships on the grounds that they reinforce patriarchal norms. In 1970, at the Second Congress to Unite Women, a group of women who protested Friedan's notion that lesbianism was a "lavender menace" in the women's movement distributed a manifesto called "The Woman-Identified Woman," which positioned lesbianism as a form of resistance to patriarchal authority. These women, who came to be known as Radicalesbians, espoused the idea that women can only be free when their personhood is independent of male cultural norms and male-defined response patterns. Radicalesbians pointed out that as long as the women's movement tries to free women without addressing the basic power dynamics of the heterosexual structure underlying the relationships between men and women, it cannot bring about women's liberation. "It is the primacy of women relating to women," reads the Radicalesbian manifesto, "of women creating a new consciousness of and with each other which is at the heart of women's liberation, and the basis for the cultural revolution" (Saraswati, 2021).

Radical feminist author and activist Andrea Dworkin, who identified as a lesbian although she was married to two men, analyzed heterosexual sex as a form of sexual subordination of women in a male-supremacist society, in which the experience of intercourse for both men and women involves the dominance and violation of women by men. Her reference to the violation of women in heterosexual sex has led to the misinterpretation of her work as claiming that all sex is rape. Dworkin disavowed this interpretation, clarifying her view that sex must be reciprocal and not an aggressive act by a man looking merely to pleasure himself.

Dworkin also railed against pornography as misogynistic dehumanization of women, arguing that pornography promotes violence against women, not only in its production but also in its consumption, which denigrates women by eroticizing their domination by men. Radical feminism has been influenced by Dworkin in holding that the only true liberation for women involves women choosing other women as romantic partners rather than engaging in patriarchal institutions such as marriage and heterosexual sex.

Of course, heterosexual women may not feel that relating to other women is a choice, given their sexual orientation; repressing their sexuality may be the only choice these women can authentically make if they want to forgo men. But bisexual women may be more likely to choose relationships with other women, consistent with their attraction to both sexes. If women who identify as heterosexual explore their sexuality more fully in the context of undermining patriarchy, they may discover that their sexual orientation is more fluid than they may have imagined, in which case they may be more open to exploring relationships with other women. Freud held that all people are by nature bisexual, and if he's right, women who forgo men may gravitate toward lesbian relationships, although it's too early to know if such a trend will take place after the 2024 election.

The election has also created tremendous fear for women. It is undeniable that patriarchy got a big boost from Trump's reelection. Many men had felt resentful at the feminist movement and at the discrimination they felt they faced with #MeToo. Many took the 2024 election as an opportunity to "put women back in their place." As an admitted sexual predator who "grabs women by the pussy" and who has been found liable for sexual abuse, Trump became a model for men who would sexually abuse women. Men now feel they have permission to denigrate and oppress women. With men emboldened to see women as second-class citizens lacking basic human rights such as bodily autonomy, many women feel threatened by misogynistic rhetoric.

In his campaign, Trump glorified the manosphere by featuring supporters such as Joe Rogan, announcer for the Ultimate Fighting Championship, and Andrew Tate, who has called himself a misogynist and king of toxic masculinity. One of Trump's biggest fans has been Nick Fuentes, a white supremacist who promotes antisemitism and misogynistic culture. Fuentes, an admitted incel (involuntarily celibate) and Holocaust denier, identifies as a Christian nationalist. His YouTube page was taken down because of his hate speech. Before the election, Trump dined with Fuentes and was criticized in the media for hosting a neo-Nazi.

On Nov. 5, Fuentes posted a misogynistic phrase on X: "Your body, my choice. Forever"—a twist on the slogan popularized by women, "My body, my choice." Fuentes's post was viewed more than 90 million times and reposted more than 35,000 times. CNN reports that later that week there was a 4,600% increase in mentions of the phrase on X. And many women on TikTok posted videos saying they had received comments with the phrase (Duffy, 2023). Many of the reposts of the phrase contained photos of Supreme Court Justice Brett Kavanaugh, a hero for men who believe that in a patriarchal society men should be able to decide whether a woman has an abortion.[11] The phrase "your body, my choice" even suggests rape threats.

Hate speech against women is on the rise since the election. On November 7, Andrew Tate posted on X: "I saw a woman crossing the road today, but I just kept my foot down. Right of way? You no longer have rights" (North, 2024).

An inspection I made of online posts about "your body, my choice" showed that men were freely calling women "bitches" and claiming victory for the manosphere after a Trump win; one post even showed a brief video of a man slapping a woman on the face. Even young girls are hearing the phrase from boys at school, and men on college campuses are insulting women with the phrase. It is not surprising, then, that women would want to turn away from men who are expressing such derision and hostility toward women and depriving them of bodily autonomy. The rise in misogynistic posts, including calls to repeal the 19th Amendment, which gives women the right to vote, suggests hard times ahead for women.

If the women's movement was facing a backlash before the last election, the backlash has escalated and threatens to push women back into the kitchen and bedroom. The election outcome reinstated male supremacy and endangered many of the gains women have made. Trump is no defender of women's rights, despite his claiming that he is the father of IVF and a protector of women, "whether they like it or not." Project 2025,

---

[11] Kavanaugh was appointed to the Supreme Court by Trump, along with Neil Gorsuch and Amy Coney Barrett, ostensibly to overturn Roe v. Wade. Kavanaugh faced opposition to the appointment as a result of charges by Christine Blasey Ford that he had sexually abused her when they were teenagers. Mr. Kavanaugh denied the allegation but was valorized by men who feel entitled to sexually violate women.

the playbook for a Trump presidency, calls for a national abortion ban. At risk, in addition to abortion procedures, are abortion pills, contraceptives, IVF, and same-sex marriage for lesbians (as well as gays). The Trump administration could very well invoke the Comstock Act of 1873 to prevent the distribution of abortion medications and supplies as well as to create a national abortion ban. And with a president who has a history of sexually abusing women, rape threats and violence against women may increase.

At the outset, this book pondered whether feminism was dead or, if not dead, then perhaps lost. Feminism has taken a real blow, and the battle lines between men and women have been drawn even more tightly. Many men, especially those making online threats to women, may consider feminism defeated. How can women pick up the pieces and move forward? Many women, deprived of reproductive rights, are literally fighting for their lives. Women are dying from the lack of reproductive health care. How can a female population unite to move feminism forward when so many women are just trying to survive?

A very real retrenchment of rights may wake women up out of complacency or stagnancy in the women's movement; women are likely to be even more motivated to fight back. The setback in rights may operate as a kickstart to reenergize a flagging feminist movement. The reaction of young women who are so angry at men that they are embracing the 4B movement in South Korea offers hope for the women's movement. If women forswear sexual relationships with men, they will not be faced with pregnancies that may require abortion access. Separatism between the sexes may help women funnel their energy into issues that promote their rights and well-being rather than expending it in relationships with men. Uniting with other women who are enraged may be productive. Rage may be the best medicine to reinvigorate feminism.

Here is where the fierce goddesses come in; they represent an archetype of female rage against injustice. If harnessed appropriately, such rage can unleash a new surge of activism. The fierce goddesses live in our collective unconscious, and as such they are present for us as long as we are willing to dive deep into the recesses of our psyches. Women who tap into the rage of the fierce goddesses will be propelled into action that reshapes society.

When Durga, Mother Goddess of the Hindu religion, was under attack by demons, Kali sprang from her forehead to defeat the demons. Kali is a fierce goddess who appeared because she was needed to protect Durga from the demons who would destroy her. Kali contains the primordial energy of the universe, which can be utilized to defeat injustice and replace it with a more equitable, life-enhancing system. Kali provides women with a model for tapping into their destructive impulses and acting on them in ways that promote a healthier society.

The demons that have arisen postelection are products of patriarchy. Men who taunt women with the phrase "Your body, my choice" and threaten them with violence are contemporary demons. Women need to look inside themselves to release the furious Kali that lives within; only then can they tap into the destructive energy needed to eradicate the patriarchal demons. Once the demons are defeated, the opportunity will arise to create a society that ensures that women can live free of misogyny and oppression. Perhaps then it will be possible to elect the first female president.

Black women are perhaps the most disaffected group as a result of the election. Ninety percent of them voted for Harris as a Black woman who could represent their interests (whereas 42% of women generally voted for Harris). As a highly marginalized group in the U.S., Black women have more difficulty accessing reproductive health care and have higher rates of maternal mortality than their white counterparts. Yet for the women's movement to be successful in promoting and achieving rights for women, white women will need to unite with Black and Brown women in an intersectional movement to defeat the demons of patriarchy.

Rage will be the common denominator that brings BIPOC and white women together to fight against misogyny and toxic masculinity. The rage of young women will hopefully be contagious for other women who find their rights curtailed under the new administration. An intersectional movement of women connecting to the energy of the fierce goddesses will bring about a new wave of feminism that will, like a phoenix, arise from the ashes of an obsolete and defeated patriarchy.

References

Alkhaldi, C. & Ebrahim, N. (2022, September 28). Grief, Protest, and Power: Why Iranian Women are Cutting their Hair. *CNN.* Grief, protest and power: Why Iranian women are cutting their hair. CNN. https://cnn.com

Archaeology (2022). https://www.archaeology.org/issues/370-2003/sidebars/8452-ireland-national-epic

Arundel, K. (2022, June 23). Study: Head Start provides opportunities to break cycle of poverty across generations. *K-12 Dive*. https://www.k12dive.com/news/study-finds-positive-outcomes-for-second-generation-of-head-start-children/625962/

Atashi, S. (2022, September 15). Women Cutting Their Hair is an Ancient Persian Tradition. *X.* https://x.com/AtashiShara/status/1572512342671503360

Barrow, K. & Panovka, R. (2022). "What To Do About Feminism." The Drift. https://www.thedriftmag.com

Begg, E. (1989). *The Cult of the Black Virgin*. Penguin.

Bible (King James version). Genesis 1:28. https://www.bible-gateway.com/passage/?search=Genesis%201%3A27-28&version=KJVBiblegateway.com

Bible Gateway, New International Version. Ephesians 5:22-33. https://www.biblegateway.com/passage/?search=Ephesians%205%3A22-33&version=NIV

Bible. (n.d.). https://blogs.https://www.Bible.org

Bipartisanpolicy. (2022, March 1). Paid Family Leave Across OECD. https://bipartisanpolicy.org/explainer/paid-family-leave-across-oecd-countries/

Birnbaum, L. (2002). *Dark Mother: African Origins and Godmothers*. iUniverse.

Boston, P.J. (2008). Gaia Hypothesis. *ScienceDirect*. https://www.sciencedirect.com/topics/earth-and-planetary-sciences/gaia-hypothesis#:~:text=Since%20the%201970s%20James%20Lovelock,it%20habitable%20for%20the%20biosphere

Brannen, C. (2023). *Entering Hecate's Cave: The Journey Through Darkness to Wholeness*. Weiser.

Brown, E., Swaine, J. & Boorstein, M. (2020, October 6). Amy Coney Barrett served as 'handmaid' in Christian group People of Praise. *The Washington Post*, https://www.washingtonpost.com/investigations/amy-coney-barrett-people-of-praise/2020/10/06/5f497d8c-0781-11eb-859b-f9c27abe638d_story.html

Burton, S. (2023, June 22). The Retrievals. *The New York Times*. https://www.nytimes.com/2023/06/22/podcasts/serial-the-retrievals-yale-fertility-clinic.html.

Chapman, B. et al. (2013, October). Emotion suppression and mortality risk over a 12-year follow-up. *Journal of Psychosomatic Research,* 75(4), 381-5. https//:doi: 10.1016/j.jpsychores.2013.07.014.

Chemaly, S. (2018). *Rage Becomes Her: The Power of Women's Anger*. Simon & Schuster.

Cherry, K. (2024). Black Madonna of Czestochowa becomes lesbian defender Erzuli Dantor. *QSpirit*. https://qspirit.net/black-madonna-lesbian-erzuli-dantor-czestochowa/

Crenshaw, K. (1989). De-Marginalizing the Intersection of Race and Sex: A Black Feminist Critique of Anti-Discrimination

Doctrine. *Feminist Theory and Antiracist Politics.* University of Chicago Legal Forum.

Culpepper, E. (1986). Ancient Gorgons: A Face for Contemporary Women's Rage. "Women of Power" magazine. Cambridge.

Davis, C. (2022, February 12). To Lose My Chronic Pain, I Had to Find My Rage. *Ms. Magazine*. https://msmagazine.com/2022/02/12/chronic-pain-women-repressed-emotions-rage/

Desai, S. (2014, March 4). Gulabi Gang: India's women warriors. *Al Jazeera*. https://www.aljazeera.com/features/2014/3/4/gulabi-gang-indias-women-warriors

Desta, Y. (2018). Viola Davis Regrets Making *The Help*: It Wasn't the Voices of the Maids That Were Heard. https://www.vanityfair.com/hollywood/2018/09/viola-davis-the-help-regret?srsltid=AfmBOopwfm-W9ZL2SSs0yyoxiKbj8KEZhG_eR5j_6G4G9cIiaAVhWRq7.

Dominus, S. (2023, February 5). A Vicious Cycle. *The New York Times.* https://www.nytimes.com/2023/02/01/magazine/menopause-hot-flashes-hormone-therapy.html

Dorsey, L. (2020). *Orishas, Goddesses, and Voodoo Queens: The Divine Feminine in the African Religious Traditions.* Weiser.

Duffy, C. (2024, November 13). *'Your body, my choice': Attacks on women surge on social media following election.* CNN. https://www.cnn.com/2024/11/11/business/your-body-my-choice-movement-election/index.html

Editors (1991, Fall). Women of Color. A Celebration of Spirit. *Journal of Liberation Publications* (21). Baltimore.

Eldred, S. (2023, April 27). Black Women Suffer Disproportionally from Menopause Symptoms. Awareness Could Help Change That. *SahanJournal*. https://sahanjournal.com/health/black-women-suffer-disproportionately-from-menopause-symptoms/

Elliott, J. (2011, April 1). The Hypocrisy of Phyllis Schlafly. *Salon.* https://www.salon.com/2011/04/01/phyllis_schlafly_child_care/

Eltahawy, M. (2022, Sept. 27). Essay: Dear White Women Cheering Iranian Women. *Feminist Giant.* https://www.feministgiant.com/p/essay-dear-white-women-cheering-iranian

Environmental Defense Fund (2024). How Climate Change Makes Hurricanes More Destructive. https://www.edf.org/climate/how-climate-change-makes-hurricanes-more-destructive

Fausto-Sterling, A. *Myths of Gender*. BasicBooks.

Figueroa, A. (2022, August 26). Jewish congregations mount legal challenges to state abortion bans. https://www.Tennesseelookout.com.

Fine, C. (2010). *Delusions of Gender.* Norton.

Flock E. (2024). *The Furies: Women, Vengeance, and Justice*. Harper Collins.

Forrest, I. (2020, June 7). Fierce Isis. *Isiopolis*. https://isiopolis.com/2020/06/07/fierce-isis-2/.

Frawley, M. (2023). African Traditional Religions: Mawu's Legacy and Women's Power in Haitian Vodou and the Diaspora. *Academia.* academia.edu/11104096/African_Traditional_Religions_Mawus_Legacy_and_Womens_Power_in_Haitian_Vodou_and_the_Diaspora?email_work_card=title

Friedan, B. (1963). *The Feminine Mystique*. W.W. Norton.

Galland, C. (1989). *Longing for Darkness: Tara and the Black Madonna*. Penguin.

Ganchimeg, E. et al. (2014). Pregnancy and Childbirth Outcomes among Adolescent Mothers: A World Health

Organization Multi-Country Study. *PubMed.* https://doi.org 10.1111/1471-0528.12630.

Gansberg, M. (1964, March 27). Apathy at Stabbing of Queens Woman Shocks Inspector. *New York Times.* https://www.nytimes.com/1964/03/27/archives/37-who-saw-murder-didnt-call-the-police-apathy-at-stabbing-of.html

Ghorayshi, A. (2021, December 20). Women Earn $2 Million Less Than Men in their Careers as Doctors. *The New York Times.* https://www.nytimes.com/2021/12/06/health/women-doctors-salary-pay-gap.html.

Gimbutas, M. (1995). *Language of the Goddess.* Harper San Francisco.

Goldberg, M. (2022, June 17). The Future Isn't Female Anymore. *The New York Times. https://www.nytimes.com/2022/06/17/opinion/roe-dobbs-abortion-feminism.html*

Goldsmith, B. & Beresford, M. (2018, June 25). India Most Dangerous Place for Women with Sexual Violence Rife. *Reuters.* https://www.reuters.com/article/world/india-most-dangerous-country-for-women-with-sexual-violence-rife-global-poll-idUSKBN1JM075/

Graves, R. (1948). *The White Goddess.* Farrar, Straus and Giroux.

Gray, J. (2012). *Men are from Mars, Women are from Venus.* Harper.

Griffith, E. (2022). *Formidable: American Women and the Fight for Equality.* Pegasus Books.

Grosz, T. (1996, December 11). *Space, Time, and Perversion.* Routledge.

Guo, K. (2023, May 29). Congress prods Biden administration on female crash dummies. *Politico.* https://www.politico.com/news/2023/05/29/new-crash-test-dummies-could-save-womens-lives-00099001

Gupta, A. (2023, August 23). How Menopause Affects Women of Color. *The New York Times.* https://www.nytimes.com/2023/08/23/well/live/menopause-symptoms-women-of-color.html

Gustafson, F. (1990). *The Black Madonna*. Sigo.

Haller, S. (2018, October 4). Daycare kids are better than those who stay at home. We know, you have thoughts. *USA Today.* https://www.usatoday.com/story/life/allthemoms/2018/10/04/daycare-kids-better-behaved-study-finds/1522045002/

Halton, M. (2018). Climate change impacts women more than men. https://www.bbc.com/news/science-environment-43294221

Harris, J. (2022, January). Do Wages Fall When Women Enter an Occupation? *ScienceDirect* (74). https://www.sciencedirect.com/science/article/abs/pii/S0927537121001378

Harrison, J. (1991). *Prolegomena to the Study of Greek Religion.* Princeton.

Harvard Health Blog. (2017, October 9). Women and Pain: Disparities in Experience and Treatment. https://www.health.harvard.edu/blog/women-and-pain-disparities-in-experience-and-treatment-2017100912562

Hawkins, D. (2019, December 31.) Amazons were long considered a myth. These discoveries show warrior women were real. *The Washington Post.* https://www.washingtonpost.com/science/2019/12/31/amazons-were-long-considered-myth-these-discoveries-show-warrior-women-were-real/

Herbert, C. (2022, May 13). Bakery sends Amber Heard a severed finger cake and vodka bottle—and it does not go down well. *Joe.* https://www.joe.co.uk/news/bakery-amber-heard-severed-finger-cake-335539

Holy Bible. (n.d.). King James' version. Genesis 2:18-21. A.J. Holman. hooks, b. (2000). *Feminist Theory: From Margin to Center* (2nd ed.). Pluto Press.

Howell, Z. (2021). Indigenous women and LGBTQ+ people led Dakota Access Pipeline protests. Five years later they reflect on Standing Rock. *THE 19th*. https://19thnews.org/2021/05/indigenous-women-and-lgbtq-people-led-dakota-access-pipeline-protests-five-years-later-they-reflect-on-standing-rock/

Hracuity (2023, August 23). Workplace Misconduct Data—Stats on Workplace Misconduct. https://www.hracuity.com/resources/research/workplace-harassment-and-employee-misconduct-insights/

Jewish Publication Society Bible. (n.d.). https://www. jps.org.

Johns, A. (2024). *Baba Yaga: The Ambiguous Mother and Witch of the Russian Folktale*. Peter Lang.

Johnston, E. (2016, November 6). The Original 'Nasty Woman.' *The Atlantic*. https://www.theatlantic.com/entertainment/archive/2016/11/the-original-nasty-woman-of-classical-myth/506591/

Jordan, J. (2007). *Some of Us Did Not Die: New and Selected Essays.* Civitas.

Kane, H. (2000). *Pele: Goddess of Hawaii's Volcanoes*. Kawainui Press.

Kaur, H. (2024, November 13). *After Trump's win, some women are considering the 4B movement*. CNN. https://www.cnn.com/2024/11/09/us/4b-movement-trump-south-korea-wellness-cec/index.html

Khan Academy (2024). American Women and World War II. https://www.khanacademy.org/humanities/us-history/rise-to-world-power/us-wwii/a/american-women-and-world-war-ii.

Kochhar, R. (2023, March 1). The Enduring Grip of the Gender Pay Gap. Pew Research Center. https://www.pewresearch.org/social-trends/2023/03/01/the-enduring-grip-of-the-gender-pay-gap/

Koltuv, B. (1986). *The Book of Lilith.* Nicolas-Hays.

Kring, S. (2016, November 29). Women are the Backbone of the Standing Rock Movement. https://time.com/4583926/standing-rock-women/

Kulasagaram, P. (2022, June 10). American sex toy maker slammed for its Amber Heard-inspired 'liquor bottle' dildo. Maylay Mail. https://www.malaymail.com/news/life/2022/06/10/american-sex-toy-maker-slammed-for-its-amber-heard-inspired-liquor-bottle-dildo/11641#google_vignette

Kutz, J. (2024). These are the climate grannies. They'll do whatever is necessary to protect their grandchildren. *THE 19th*. https://19thnews.org/2024/01/climate-grandmothers-environmental-activism/

Lilly Ledbetter (2024, November 7). In Wikipedia. https://en.wikipedia.org/wiki/Lilly_Ledbetter

Longmire. B. (2023). Jessica Chastain Takes Swipe at Oscars for Snubbing Viola Davis and 'The Woman King' at 2023 Ceremony. https://www.imdb.com/news/ni64054712.

Lorde, A. (2007). The Uses of Anger. Women Responding to Racism. *Sister Outsider: Essays and Speeches by Audre Lorde.* Crossing Press.

Lovelock, J. (2021, November 2). Beware: Gaia may destroy humans before we can destroy the Earth. *The Guardian.* www.theguardian.com/commentisfree/2021/nov/02/beware-gaia-theory-climate-crisis-earth

Malhi, G. & Mann, J. (2018, November 24). Depression. *The Lancet Psychiatry*, 4(2), 146-158. https://www.thelancet.com/journals/lancet/article/PIIS0140-6736(18)31948-2

March of Dimes (2020, January 10). Long-term economic benefit of paid family leave. https://www.marchofdimes.org/find-support/blog/long-term-economic-benefit-paid-family-leave.

Marsh, J., Brett, K., & Miller, L. (1999). Racial Differences in Hormone Replacement Therapy Prescriptions. *Science Direct*, 93(6), 999-1003. https://doi.org/10.1016/S0029-7844(98)00540-7

Miller, C. (2016, March 20). As Women Take Over a Male-Dominated Field, the Pay Drops. *The New York Times*. https://www.nytimes.com/2016/03/20/upshot/as-women-take-over-a-male-dominated-field-the-pay-drops.html.

Molinari, S. & Brooke, B. (2021, December 21). Women are more likely to be injured in car crashes. Here are the reasons why. *The Washington Post*. https://www.washingtonpost.com/opinions/2021/12/21/female-crash-test-dummies-nhtsa/

Nandi, S. (2017, March 8). Expert take: Making unpaid work visible creates livelihood for rural women. www.unwomen.org/en/news/stories/2017/3/experts-take-subhalakshmi-nandi-unpaid-work

Napikoski, L. (2019, February 28). Lavender Menace: The Phrase, the Group, the Controversy. ThoughtCo. https://www.thoughtco.com/lavender-menace-feminism-definition-3528970

Narayan, D. (2018). *Chup: Breaking the Silence about India's Women*. Juggernaut Publication.

National Head Start Association. (2022, December). Benefits of Head Start and Early Head Start Programs. https://headstartva.org/wp-content/uploads/2022/12/BenefitsofHSandEHS.pdf

National Institute of Health (2024, October 21). N.I.H. Policy and Guidelines on the Inclusion of Women and Minorities as Subjects in Clinical Research. https://

grants.nih.gov/policy-and-compliance/policy-topics/inclusion/women-and-minorities/guideline#:~:text=It%20is%20the%20policy%20of,that%20inclusion%20is%20inappropriate%20with

Neff, K., Smith, S. & Pieper, K. (2022, March). Inequality Across 1,500 Popular Films: Examining Gender and Race/Ethnicity of Leads/Co Leads from 2007-2021. Annenberg Foundation. https://assets.uscannenberg.org/docs/aii-study-inequality-popular-films-20220311.pdf

Nimmo, H. (2011). *Pele: Volcano Goddess of Hawaii.* McFarland.

North, A. (2024, November 13). *"Your body, my choice": The misogynist MAGA attack, explained.* Vox. https://www.vox.com/politics/384792/your-body-my-choice-maga-gender-election

Obama White House Archives. (2013). Fact Sheet: Key Provisions in the Violence Against Women Act. https://www.Obamawhitehouse.archives.gov

Office on Women's Health. (2023). Disparities and the Leading Causes of Death in Women - National Women's Health Week. U.S. Department of Health and Human Services. https://www.womenshealth.gov/node/1374

Outlook. (2022, September 30). Supreme Court's Observations 'Welcome' but Marital Rape Still Not Illegal in India: Here are Countries Where It Is. https://www.outlookindia.com/national/sc-observations-welcome-but-omarital-rape-still-not-illegal-in-india-here-are-countries-where-it-is-news-226913

Oxford English Dictionary, languages.oup.com. n.d.

Pappas, S. (2012, April 9). Doctors Appalled by 10-Year-Old giving Birth. https://www.livescience.com

Patai, R. (1990). *The Hebrew Goddess* (3rd ed.). Wayne State University.

Perez, C. (2021). *Invisible Women.* Harry N. Abrams.

Pew Research (2024, May 13). Broad Public Support for Legal Abortion Persists 2 Years After Dobbs. https://www.pewresearch.org

Pillemer, K., Munsch, C., Fuller-Rowell, T., Riffin, C. & Suitor, J. (2012, October). Ambivalence Toward Adult Children: Differences Between Mothers and Fathers, *Journal of Marriage and Family,* 74(5). https://doi: 10.1111/j.1741-3737.2012.01004.x

Ramaswamy, S. (2013, October 13). Fatherhood premium, motherhood penalty? What Nobel Prize economics winner's research shows. *USA Today*. https://www.usatoday.com/story/money/2023/10/13/claudia-goldin-gender-wage-gap-parents/71128533007/

RealMermaids. (2024). Mami Wata. http://www.realmermaids.net/mermaid-legends/mami-wata/

Reichard, J. (2015). *Pele: Hawaiian Goddess of the Volcano.* Create Space.

Reimers, A (2017). *Not Reliable Guides: An analysis of some covenant community structures.* LAP Lambert.

Rose, D. (1996). Black Madonnas: from Ancient Dark Ancestress to Blessed Virgin Mary. *Goddessing.*

Rosenblatt, K. (2022, April 27). Johnny Depp and Amber Heard Defamation Trial: Summary and Timeline. *NBC News.* https://www.nbcnews.com/pop-culture/pop-culture-news/johnny-depp-amber-heard-defamation-trial-summary-timeline-rcna26136

Rupp J., Winant, F. et al. (1978). Power. *Women: a Journal of Liberation*, vol 6, (1).

San Francisco Museum of Mutant History (2011, July). *Marvel.* https://marvel.fandom.com/wiki/Museum_of_Mutant_History

Sandy, M. (2019, September). The Amazon Rain Forest is Nearly Gone. https://time.com/amazon-rainforest-disappearing/

Saraswati, L., Shaw, B. & Rellihan, H. (2021). The Woman-Identified Woman. *Introduction to Women's, Gender & Sexuality Studies*. Oxford.

Saraswati, L., Shaw, B., & Rellihan, H. (2021). The Gender Pay Gap. *Introduction to Women's, Gender & Sexuality Studies.* Oxford.

Sauro, D. (2023, November 25). The Secret to Enrolling More Women in Clinical Research. *Pharmaphorum*. https://pharmaphorum.com/market-access/secret-enrolling-more-women-clinical-research

Seresin, A. (2019, October 9). On Heteropessimism. *The New Inquiry*. https://thenewinquiry.com/on-heteropessimism/

Shaver, K. (2012, March 7). Female dummy makes her mark on male-dominated crash tests. *The Washington Post.* (https://www.washingtonpost.com/local/trafficandcommuting/female-dummy-makes-her-mark-on-male-dominated-crash-tests/2012/03/07/gIQANBLjaS_story.html

Shokoohi, K. (2021, January 11). The 2,000-year-old Wonder Women who inspired the comic. *BBC*. www.bbc.com/culture/article/20210111-the-ancient-roots-of-wonder-woman

Smith, M. (2023, October 10). Novel Prize-winning Harvard economist Claudia Goldin: The gender pay gap will never close unless this happens. *Cnbc*. https://www.cnbc.com/2023/10/10/nobel-prize-winner-claudia-goldin-the-gender-pay-gap-will-never-close-unless-this-happens.html

Solly, M. (2022, September 15). The Real Warriors Behind 'The Woman King.' *Smithsonian Magazine*. https://www.smithsonianmag.com/history/real-warriors-woman-king-dahomey-agojie-amazons-180980750/#:~:text=As%20 historian%20Robin%20Law%20notes,monumental%20 scale%20of%20Dahomey's%20warfare.

Southern Poverty Law Center. (2022, June 1). "SPLC Poll Finds Substantial Support for 'Great Replacement' Theory and Other Hard-Right Ideas." https://www.splc,org

Starhawk. (1999). *The Spiral Dance.* HarperSanFrancisco.

Statista (2022). https://www.statista.com/aboutus/our-research-commitment.

Summers, J. (2023, October 25). Gender inequality protesters in Iceland refused to do work for a day—even childcare. N*PR.* https://www.npr.org/2023/10/25/1208577504/gender-inequality-protesters-in-iceland-refused-to-do-work-for-a-day-even-childcare

The University of Alabama at Birmingham (2022). Witchcraft, Women, & the Healing Arts in the Early Modern Period: Female Midwives. *UAB Libraries.* https://guides.library.uab.edu/c.php?g=1048546&p=7609202

Thomas, L. (2022). *The Intersectional Environmentalist. How to Dismantle Systems of Oppression to Protect People + Planet.* Voracious Press.

U. S. Department of Health and Human Services (2024, June 30). Head Start Services. https://www.acf.hhs.gov/ohs/about/head-start.

UNWomen (2017, February 28). In Uruguay, care law catalyzes change, ushering services and breaking stereotypes. https://www.unwomen.org/en/news/stories/2017/2/feature-uruguay-care-law.

Walter, S. (2023, June 29). They Followed Doctors' Orders. Then Their Children Were Taken Away. *New York Times.* https://www.nytimes.com/2023/06/29/magazine/pregnant-women-medication-suboxonbabies.html

Weber, C. (2019). *The Morrigan: Celtic Goddess of Magick and Might*. Weiser.

Weber, C. (2021). *Hekate: Goddess of Witches*. Weiser.

Wilk, S. (2007). *Medusa: Solving the Mystery of the Gorgon*. Oxford.

World Health Organization (2024, March 25). Violence against women. https://www.who.int/news-room/fact-sheets/detail/violence-against-women#:~:text=Globally%20as%20many%20as%2038,sexual%20violence%20are%20more%20limited.

World Population Review (2024). Marital Rape States. https://worldpopulationreview.com/state-rankings/marital-rape-states

Yamata (2023, March 1). Oscars diversity improved after #OscarsSoWhite, study shows. But glaring gaps remain. Los Angeles Times. https://www.latimes.com/entertainment-arts/movies/story/2023-03-01/oscars-diversity-usc-annenberg-inclusion-initiative-academy-oscars-so-white#:~:text=Looking%20at%20the%20eight%20years,that%20number%20increased%20to%2017%25.

Young, M. (2021, February 18). Thank You, Rush Limbaugh, For My Feminism. *Ms Magazine.* https://msmagazine.com/2021/02/18/rush-limbaugh-dead-women-feminism-feminazi/

Zambelich, A & Alexandra, C. (2016, December 11). In Their Own Words: The 'Water Protectors' of Standing Rock. https://www.npr.org/2016/12/11/505147166/in-their-own-words-the-water-protectors-of-standing-rock

Index

F

G

www.ingramcontent.com/pod-product-compliance
Lightning Source LLC
LaVergne TN
LVHW052302200926
848481LV00002B/444